8 WEEKS OF
LOVE

8 Weeks of Love: A Bible Study for Single Mothers

Copyright © 2016 by Lois M. Breit

ISBN-13: 978-1533204554

ISBN-10: 1533204551

Editing by Sarah R. Young and Emily Harris

Special thanks to Heather Pepin King

Publishing and Design Services | MelindaMartin.me

Scripture quotations are from the New International Version (NIV), New Living Translation (NLT), and the Message (MSG).

Printed in the United States of America

8 WEEKS OF LOVE

A BIBLE STUDY FOR SINGLE MOTHERS

LOIS BREIT

1 Corinthians 13:4–8 (NIV): Love is patient, love is kind. It does not envy, it does not boast, it is not proud. It does not dishonor others, it is not self-seeking, it is not easily angered, it keeps no record of wrongs. Love does not delight in evil but rejoices with the truth. It always protects, always trusts, always hopes, always perseveres. Love never fails...

Study: This book is designed for a group setting or for individual study.

Footnotes: Footnotes direct you to the back of the book for leadership suggestions and Scriptural answers for those studying individually.

Contents

Introduction

This study will look at love from God's perspective because "God is Love," and He designed us to love and be loved from the time of our conception. A child, like an adult, may survive without love, but they will not thrive.

We find God's description of love in 1 Corinthians 13:4–8. Over the next eight weeks we will study what this means for you today. Week-by-week you will gain an understanding of how God's love impacts the way we love others and ourselves. You'll discover a love that heals your past, protects your present, and prepares you for your future. This study is about a life of love whether you marry or remain single.

Stories: The stories shared in this study are true, however all names have been changed.

Week One:
Love Revealed

Love Never Fails

God's Love Is Where It All Begins

God reveals His love for mankind through the scriptures. From Genesis to Revelation, He describes His love, how we should love others, and how His love never fails. First Corinthians 13 is a description of how God loves us, and is His example of how when we love each other in this way *love never fails.*

To begin our biblical search for the meaning of His love, we need to be honest with our current beliefs and feelings.

Leader Note [1]

Let's start by answering a few questions that will help you find your starting point on this biblical love quest.

Leader Note [2]

Answering these simple questions will help determine your love gauge. There are no right or wrong answers, only truthful views of how you see yourself and what you expect love to look like.

1. *Do you feel you have value as an individual (not just as a mom)? Why or why not?*

    _____

    _____

2. *Do you deserve to be loved? Why or why not?*

    _____

    _____

3. *Where does your feeling of worth generally come from? Is that an accurate source?*

_____

_____

4. *What makes you feel loved?*

_____

_____

5. *When was the last time you felt loved?*

_____

_____

6. *Do you allow yourself to love others (not including your children)? Why or why not?*

_____

_____

7. *Do you believe God loves you? Why or why not?*

_____

_____

8. *On a scale of 0-10, how much do you feel He loves you?*

_____

_____

9. *If you picked a low number, did you think God loved you at one time? What changed your belief?*

_____

_____

The best source to study and understand what love should look like comes from the creator of love, God himself. Keep in mind as we progress through the next few weeks that we were created to love and be loved from the time of our birth. God describes the characteristics of love, its passion, its strengths and its weakness throughout the entire Bible. That's why the Bible is our guidebook for this study.

The following scriptures will help us understand what love is — and what it is not.

Read Psalm 139: 1-16

> *Psalm 139: 13-14 (NIV): For You created my inmost being; You knit me together in my mother's womb. I praise You because I am fearfully and wonderfully made.*

Now personalize this by putting your name in place of the underlined words:

For You created _____ inmost being; You knit _____ together in _____ mother's womb. _____ praise You because _____ am fearfully and wonderfully made.

10. *According to these scriptures, especially verses 13-14, why are you special and loved in God's eyes?* [3]

_____

_____

Read the following verses and answer the questions.

*1 John 3:1 (NIV): See what great love the Father has **lavished** on us, that we should be called children of God! And that is what we are!*

11. *What relationship do we have with God?* [4]

_____

_____

Matthew 7:9-11 (NIV): Which of you, if your son asks for bread, will give him a stone? Or if he asks for a fish, will give him a snake? If you, then, though you are evil, know how to give good gifts to your children, how much more will your Father in heaven give good gifts to those who ask him!

12. *According to this passage, does God want to bless you? How often?*

_____

_____

John 3:16 (NIV): For God so loved the world that He gave His one and only Son, that whoever believes in Him shall not perish, but have eternal life.

Romans 5:8 (NIV): But God demonstrates His own love for us in this: While we were still sinners, Christ died for us.

13. *What motivated God to make such a huge sacrifice for you? Hint: It's only one word.*

_____

_____

Read all of Luke 15:11-31. It tells the story of a son who left home in rebellion to live life his own way, rejecting his father's love, provision, and legacy for success. It's also the story of a father's unfailing love and restorative power.

Luke 15:21-24 (NIV): The son said to him, "Father, I have sinned against heaven and against you. I am no longer worthy to be called your son." But the father said to his servants, "Quick! Bring the best robe and put it on him. Put a ring on his finger and sandals on his feet. Bring the fattened calf and kill it. Let's have a feast and celebrate. For this son of mine was dead and is alive again; he was lost and is found." So they began to celebrate.

14. *Is this "prodigal son" like you in any way? How?*

_____

_____

15. *Has your stubbornness or selfish choices caused you or others unnecessary pain?*

_____

_____

16. *What did the son do to gain restoration with his father?* [5]

_____

_____

17. *Do you believe God desires to welcome you with open arms?*

_____

_____

Our selfish behavior, running from God and making wrong choices, does not kill God's love for us. He waits and watches for us to return to Him so He can celebrate with us, not so He can punish us!

We always see this story as "The Prodigal Son," but it could easily be called "The Father's Love." He loved his foolish, rebellious son even when his love, provision, and future inheritance were rejected and squandered. The father patiently waited for his son to return, lavishly welcomed him home, and lovingly restored him to the family.

If you are the prodigal returning home to the Father and the church, remember the father welcomed him, but the brother did not. The father had to remind the brother that his hard work and long-standing love would always be rewarded, but indignation and jealousy over the return of the prodigal brother was not the proper response.

In other words, some people in the church may at first say hurtful words or not immediately become your friend, but don't let them keep you away! Let God speak to their hearts while you enjoy the love of the Father.

Read the following verses and answer the questions.

> *Romans 8:38-39 (NIV): For I am convinced that neither death nor life, neither angels nor demons, neither the present nor the future, nor any powers, neither height nor depth, nor anything else in all creation, will be able to separate us from the love of God that is in Christ Jesus our Lord.*

18. *According to this scripture, is there anything that can separate you from the Father's love?* [6]

_____

_____

> *Ephesians 2:8-9 (NIV): For it is by grace you have been saved, through faith—and this is not from yourselves, it is the gift of God— not by works, so that no one can boast.*

> *1 John 1:9 (NIV): If we confess our sins, He is faithful and just and will forgive us our sins and purify us from all unrighteousness.*

> *Matthew 7:7 (NIV): Ask and it will be given to you; seek and you will find; knock and the door will be opened to you.*

19.   *What's required to receive the blessings that come from God's love?* [7]

_____

_____

Numbers 23:19 (NLT): God is not a man, so he does not lie. He is not human, so he does not change his mind...

20.   *Why is it unfair to compare God to an earthly father?* [8]

_____

_____

Song of Solomon 2:4 (NIV): ... let His banner over me be love.

In biblical times, banners were raised high to encourage and rally the troops, especially during a battle. God's banner of love over us means we are His and that He has the victory over our brokenness, defeats, hurts, and fears. His love for us never fails.

21.   *Do you now believe God loves you? How much on a scale of 0-10?*

_____

_____

Hopefully your self-rating has risen this week.

Lois' Journey: When I began my journey as a broken, confused, abandoned mother of five, my thoughts and understanding of love was a jumble of falsehoods and emotions.

I felt abandoned by God, forgotten, and unloved. Romans 8:38-39 seemed foreign to me. How could God possibly love me when I didn't even like me? I routinely recounted my failures each night to underscore why I had been rejected and abandoned by my husband. I constantly thought, if only I could change who I am, I could be loved. But one night God interrupted my routine and said "Lois, even if you never changed from this moment on, My love for you will never change".

This scripture, and the others we studied this week, helped me understand a love that wasn't based on who I was or what I did, but on who God is. His unconditional love will never be rescinded even if we reject it. God's love never fails, even when ours may fall short.

If you have not yet accepted this love that is so generously offered to you, this is your opportunity to do so. Praying this simple prayer is all it takes:

Father God, forgive me for my sins, my past, my stubbornness, and my rejection of Your love. I believe Jesus died on the cross for me, and I accept your love today. Nothing can ever separate me from it again. I pray this in the name of Jesus, amen.

Challenge: Memorize at least one verse from this week's study that will be a reminder of how God revealed His love to you.

Notes & Reflections

The scripture I chose to memorize this week:

_____

_____

_____

_____

_____

Why I chose it:

_____

_____

_____

_____

_____

Love Changes Everything!

Week Two: Your Love for God, Part I

Love is Not Self-Seeking

Love Is Not a One-Way Street

In week one, we established that God loves you unconditionally. This week, we'll look at how to keep a love relationship two-sided and strong, which is necessary for any healthy relationship.

> *Deuteronomy 6:4-5 (NIV): . . . Love the Lord your God with all your heart and with all your soul and with all your strength.*

God was preparing the Israelites for the blessings and temptations they would face as they entered into the Promised Land and their future.

Modern Jews still recite this verse every morning and evening as a reminder to love God above the temptations of the day and to continuously pursue Him.

This verse is repeated throughout the Bible as a reminder to keep our love of God fresh and above all of the problems and distractions that try to interrupt our relationship with Him. To love God with all our heart, mind and soul remains the foundation of our peace, joy, and love—the natural result of passionately putting Him first.

How do we love God with such fervor, especially if we are afraid to love at all?

Read the following verses and answer the questions.

> *1 John 4:18 (NIV): There is no fear in love; but perfect love casts out fear, because fear involves punishment, and the one who fears is not perfected in love.*

1 John 4:19 (NIV): We love because he first loved us.

God's love is perfect—when we fully love God, we fully trust Him, and fear no longer rules our lives. Understanding the power of God's love enables us to love the One who loves us so unconditionally.

1. *Have you ever felt God has let you down or abandoned you? In what ways?*

   _____

   _____

2. *Have you gotten mad at God or blamed Him for bad things that have happened to you?*

   _____

   _____

3. *Has any good or—peace—come from blaming God for your problems?*

   _____

   _____

4. *Do you express your love to God on a daily basis? If so, how?*

   _____

   _____

God mentions the importance of loving Him throughout the scriptures. Here are just a few examples:

> *Deuteronomy 11:13-15 (NIV): So if you faithfully obey the commands I am giving you today—to love the Lord your God and to serve Him with all your heart and with all your soul—then I will send rain on your land in its season, both autumn and spring rains, so that you may gather in your grain, new wine and olive oil. I will provide grass in the fields for your cattle, and you will eat and be satisfied.*

Notice how promises and blessings follow.

> *Deuteronomy 13:2-4 (NIV): . . . and the [false] prophet says, "Let us follow other gods and let us worship them"—you must not listen to the words of that prophet or dreamer. The Lord your God is testing you to find out whether you love Him with all your heart and with all your soul. It is the Lord your God you must follow, and Him you must revere. Keep His commands and obey Him; serve Him and hold fast to Him.*

God knows others will try to lead you away from Him.

> *Deuteronomy 30:6 (NIV): The Lord your God will circumcise your hearts and the hearts of your descendants, so that you may love Him with all your heart and with all your soul, and live.*

Circumcision of the heart means to be purified and separated unto God.

> *Joshua 22:5 (NIV): But be very careful to keep the commandment and the law that Moses the servant of the Lord gave you: to love the Lord your God, to walk in obedience to Him, to keep His commands, to hold fast to Him and to serve Him with all your heart and with all your soul.*
>
> *Matthew 22:37 (NIV): Jesus replied: "'Love the Lord your God with all your heart and with all your soul and with all your mind." This is the first and greatest commandment.*
>
> *Mark 12:30 (NIV): Love the Lord your God with all your heart and with all your soul and with all your mind and with all your strength.*
>
> *Luke 10:27 (NIV): Love the Lord your God with all your heart and with all your soul and with all your strength and with all your mind.*

Now that it's clear God desires we love Him just as He loves us—in a two-way relationship—let's look at how we love God.

LOVING GOD

First Corinthians 13 reminds us of several ways to express love through service, sacrifice, faithfulness, honesty, kindness, etc. But over the next two weeks we will study three basic expressions of heartfelt love that bond our relationship with God—praise, worship and obedience. Think about how these expressions of love work with people, as well as with God. This week we will focus on praise.

PRAISE

> *Psalm 89:1 (NIV): I will sing of the Lord's great love forever; with my mouth I will make Your faithfulness known through all generations.*

Praise is good boasting. It's about the words we speak to someone or about someone—in this case God. It's a verbal expression of love and gratitude. It expounds on God's attributes of faithfulness, patience, forgiveness, and our trust in Him. Praising God establishes a positive focus! It keeps our eyes and thoughts on God, all He has done, and all He is able to do.

King David had an unashamed love of God. He hid nothing from God, and he praised God through his fears, victories, criticism, and failures. Praise cemented their relationship of *mutual* love.

> *1 Samuel 13:14 (NIV): . . . the Lord has sought out a man after His own heart and appointed him ruler of His people.*

The following scriptures show how praise brings joy to God, raises our confidence, and builds a strong love relationship. King David wrote many of these scriptures on his journey from boyhood to great king. David was called "a man after

God's own heart." David's love for God is an example for us to follow. Even in his imperfections, David's love for God never wavered.

God is being praised in each of the following scriptures. You may need to read the surrounding verses to better understand the situation, discover the victory, and find today's application for your life. After reading the verse(s), list the circumstance, result, and personal reminder from each.

Example: *1 Samuel 17:37 (NIV): The Lord who rescued me from the paw of the lion and the paw of the bear will rescue me from the hand of this Philistine.*

Circumstance:

David, the teenager, was facing a huge foe with overwhelming odds against him. His praise focused on what God could do, instead of what David was unable to do on his own

Result:

Praising God for his past victories in dangerous situations gave David the confidence to face another "giant" of a problem.

Reminder:

When I face a scary situation, I need to remind myself that God is with me, He is able, and I will put my trust in Him.

2 Samuel 6:20-23 (NLT): When David returned home to bless his own family, Michal, the daughter of Saul, came out to meet him. She said in disgust, "How distinguished the king of Israel looked today, shamelessly exposing himself to the servant girls like any vulgar person might do!" David retorted to Michal, "I was dancing before the Lord, who chose me above your father and all his family! He appointed me as the leader of Israel, so I celebrate before the Lord. Yes, and I am willing to look even more foolish than this, even to be humiliated in my own eyes! But those servant girls you mentioned will indeed think I am distinguished!" So Michal, the daughter of Saul, remained childless throughout her entire life.

Circumstance: [9]

_____

_____

_____

Result: [10]

_____

_____

_____

Reminder: [11]

_____

_____

_____

2 Samuel 22:4 (NIV): I called to the Lord, who is worthy of praise, and have been saved from my enemies.

Circumstance: [12]

_____

_____

_____

_____

Result: [13]

_____

_____

_____

_____

Reminder: [14]

_____

_____

_____

_____

1 Kings 8:15 (NIV): Then he said: "Praise be to the Lord, the God of Israel, who with His own hand has fulfilled what He promised with His own mouth to my father David."

Circumstance: [15]

_____

_____

_____

_____

Result: [16]

_____

_____

_____

_____

Reminder: [17]

_____

_____

_____

_____

2 Chronicles 20:21 (NIV): After consulting the people, Jehoshaphat appointed men to sing to the Lord and to praise Him for the splendor of His holiness as they went out at the head of the army, saying: "Give thanks to the Lord, for His love endures forever."

(Read also 2 Chronicles 20:29-30).

Circumstance: [18]

_____

_____

_____

_____

Result: [19]

_____

_____

_____

_____

Reminder: [20]

_____

_____

_____

Psalm 16:7 (NIV): I will praise the Lord, who counsels me; even at night my heart instructs me.

Circumstance: [21]

_____

_____

_____

_____

Result: [22]

_____

_____

_____

_____

Reminder: [23]

_____

_____

_____

_____

Psalm 28:6-7 (NIV): Praise be to the Lord, for He has heard my cry for mercy. The Lord is my strength and my shield; my heart trusts in Him, and He helps me. My heart leaps for joy, and with my song I praise Him.

Circumstance: [24]

_____

_____

_____

_____

Result: [25]

_____

_____

_____

_____

Reminder: [26]

_____

_____

_____

_____

Psalm 42:5 (NIV): Why, my soul, are you downcast? Why so disturbed within me? Put your hope in God, for I will yet praise Him, my Savior and my God.

Circumstance: [27]

_____

_____

_____

_____

Result: [28]

_____

_____

_____

_____

Reminder: [29]

_____

_____

_____

_____

Psalm 59:17 (NIV): You are my strength, I sing praise to You; You, God, are my fortress, my God on whom I can rely.

Circumstance: [30]

_____

_____

_____

_____

Result: [31]

_____

_____

_____

_____

Reminder: [32]

_____

_____

_____

_____

Psalm 66:20 (NIV): Praise be to God, who has not rejected my prayer or withheld His love from me!

Circumstance: [33]

_____

_____

_____

_____

Result: [34]

_____

_____

_____

_____

Reminder: [35]

_____

_____

_____

_____

There are over 150 references to praising God in the Bible. Praise is important to God and a mountain-mover for us! If you need to build a positive praise life, read these verses on praise: Psalm 8:2, Psalm 9:2, Psalm 18:3, Psalm 31:21, Psalm 63:4, Psalm 69:34, Psalm 96:2, Psalm 100:4, and Psalm 103:1-4.

Praise prepares our heart to be open to God. It's an expression of our gratitude, and it takes away our fear as we focus on God's abilities instead of our inadequacies. I spent a lot of time on this because I tend to complain to God much more than I praise Him. In doing so, I miss out on the blessings of a two-way relationship with Him: peace, joy, forgiveness, protection, provision, and victories!

5.   *What reason(s) do you have to praise God today?*

_____

_____

6.   *In what ways will praising God help you love others in the future?* [36]

_____

_____

Lois' Journey: After my husband left me, I felt God had also abandoned me. I set my heart like stone against love, except for my children. I didn't even realize how limited that love had become because I'd blocked love's source.

When I quit feeling sorry for myself, and being mad at God for my situation, life changed for me. I began to praise God for providing food and shelter for my family. Instead of crying over the community we left behind, I praised Him for the new friends He brought into my life and quit mourning the loss of old ones. I praised Him for a church that was a refuge for us, a safe place to heal and be loved, replacing the isolation and rejection we'd come from. Praise softened my heart and returned my hope.

Challenge: Begin to spend one minute each morning speaking words of praise to God—out loud.

Notes & Reflections

What reasons have you found to praise God today?

_____

_____

_____

_____

_____

Which praise verses are you choosing to speak out each day?

_____

_____

_____

_____

_____

Love Changes Everything!

Week Three:
Your Love for God,
Part II

Love is Not Self-seeking

Love Is Not a One-Way Street

> *Deuteronomy 6:4-5 (NIV): . . . Love the Lord your God with all your heart and with all your soul and with all your strength.*

Last week we began our study of loving God with **praise**, one of the three basic expressions of love that bind us together with Him. We discovered the power of praise in our relationship with God and how it affects our personal relationships as well. We learned how praise releases us from anger and bitterness, changes our attitudes and outlooks, gives us hope in desperate situations, and prepares us for a life of love and victory. When our love relationship with God is strong, it brings health and joy to our personal relationships.

Discuss with your group something new you personally discovered through your one "minute of praise" challenge.

This week we continue our study of loving God through our expressions of worship and obedience.

WORSHIP

There is a difference between praise and worship. Praise is an exuberant expression of thanksgiving. It is an outward reflection of love expressed in songs, dance, words, and attitude.

Worship is the reverent acknowledgement of the power and lordship of God and humbling yourself before Him.

The dictionary describes *worship* as *an adoring reverence or regard.* This means you think about this person or thing often during your day. It will occupy your mind, it will garner the majority of your attention, and it will be the focus of your goals.

1. *What is it that you adore, or give high regard to everyday? Your looks, your children, your job, your talent, something else?*

_____

_____

Read the following scriptures on worship and think about why and how the people are worshipping God with their words and actions.

The Passover: Worship His Protection

Exodus 12:23-27 (NIV): . . . and He will not permit the destroyer to enter your houses and strike you down . . . Then the people bowed down and worshiped."

2. *Has God ever protected you?*

_____

_____

The Deliverer: Worship His mercy

> *Exodus 3:12 (NIV): And God said, "I will be with you. And this will be the sign to you that it is I who have sent you: When you have brought the people out of Egypt, you will worship God on this mountain."*

3. *Have you been freed from a situation, attitude, or behavior?*

_____

_____

His Presence: Worship His Closeness

> *Exodus 34:8 (NIV): Moses bowed to the ground at once and worshiped.*

4. *Have you experienced the presence of God?*

_____

_____

The Blessing: Worship His Love

> *Deuteronomy 5:8-10 (NIV): "You shall not make for yourself an image in the form of anything in heaven above or on the earth beneath or in the waters below. You shall not bow down to them or worship them; for I, the Lord your God, am a jealous God, punishing*

the children for the sin of the parents to the third and fourth generation of those who hate me, but showing love to a thousand generations of those who love me and keep my commandments.

We are to worship God alone! Generational bondages can be broken, and blessings can follow worship.

5.   *Do you have a generational bondage or family pattern that you would like to break?*

_____

_____

His Majesty: Worship His Position

Matthew 2:11 (NIV): On coming to the house, they saw the child with His mother Mary, and they bowed down and worshiped him.

Even kings bowed down to the Lordship of Jesus.

6.   *Do you acknowledge and worship Jesus as your Lord?*

_____

_____

The Worshippers: Worship with Sincerity

> *John 4:23 (NIV): Yet, a time is coming and has now come when the true worshipers will worship the Father in the Spirit and in truth, for they are the kind of worshipers the Father seeks.*

7. *Do you worship God from your heart and truly love Him?*

_____

_____

The Worshippers: Worship with Your Body

> *Romans 12:1 (NIV): Therefore, I urge you, brothers and sisters, in view of God's mercy, to offer your bodies as a living sacrifice, holy and pleasing to God—this is your true and proper worship.*

8. *Do you honor your body as a form of worship (keeping your sexual life pure, staying free of drugs and other harmful choices)?*

_____

_____

God desires worship because it's an expression of true love and devotion. Worship directs our attention and the flow of our hearts desires toward God, the one we love. Remember, we receive His best when the relationship goes both ways.

9.   *What have you learned about worship that you didn't realize before this study?*

_____

_____

10.   *How can worshipping God help your other relationships?* [37]

_____

_____

OBEDIENCE

It may seem odd to add obedience to our study on loving God. But think about how you feel when your children refuse to obey you. Do you feel alienated when they ignore your words of guidance or reject your love? Can you shower them with gifts when they are rebellious and disobedient? Is there respect in the act of disobedience? God the father desires to bless us as well, and obedience is our doorway to receive from Him.

> *Deuteronomy 10:12-13 (NIV): And now, Israel, what does the Lord your God ask of you but to fear the Lord your God, to walk in obedience to Him, to love Him, to serve the Lord your God with all your heart and with all your soul, and to observe the Lord's commands and decrees that I am giving you today for your own good?*

41

Deuteronomy 28:2 (NIV): All these blessings will come on you and accompany you if you obey the Lord your God.

Read the list of blessings that come from obedience in Deuteronomy 28: 3-14.

11.   *Which of these blessings do you need most today?*

_____

_____

12.   *What advantage is there to living in obedience to God?* [38]

_____

_____

I could list the curses that come from disobedience, but I'd rather focus on our new walk of obedience. Read Deuteronomy 28:15-64 if you want to see the results of disobedience to God.

Read the following verses and identify the result of obedience found in each one.

1 Kings 3:14 (NIV): And if you walk in obedience to Me and keep My decrees and commands as David your father did, I will give you a long life.

13.   *Result of obedience:* [39]

_____

_____

Psalm 128:1-2 (NIV): Blessed are all who fear the Lord, who walk in obedience to Him. You will eat the fruit of your labor; blessings and prosperity will be yours.

14.   *Reason for obedience:* [40]

_____

_____

John 8:31-32 (NIV): If you hold to My teaching, you are really My disciples. Then you will know the truth, and the truth will set you free.

15.   *Reason for obedience:* [41]

_____

_____

Romans 16:19 (NIV): Everyone has heard about your obedience, so I rejoice because of you; but I want you to be wise about what is good, and innocent about what is evil.

16.   *Reason for obedience:* [42]

_____

_____

2 John 1:6 (NIV): And this is love: that we walk in obedience to His commands. As you have heard from the beginning, His command is that you walk in love.

17. How is love connected to obedience in this scripture? [43]

_____

_____

18. List at least three meaningful results of obedience to God: [44]

_____

_____

_____

Disobedience is Contrary to Love

1 Samuel 15:22 (NIV): But Samuel replied: "Does the Lord delight in burnt offerings and sacrifices as much as in obeying the Lord? To obey is better than sacrifice, and to heed is better than the fat of rams. For rebellion is like the sin of divination, and arrogance like the evil of idolatry. Because you have rejected the word of the Lord, He has rejected you as king."

19. To what is disobedience (or rebellion) compared? [45]

_____

_____

20.   *What are the results of a relationship with God without obedience?* [46]

_____

_____

21.   *How important is obedience in a love relationship?* [47]

_____

_____

Remember, "God is love," so we need not fear obedience to Him.

> Lois' Journey: My praise turned to worship for a God who could love me, rescue me, and had the power to heal me. I wanted to obey the God I'd learned to trust, believing He had my best interest at heart, even when I couldn't see it at the time. My family has been blessed in more ways than I can count and I believe it's because I didn't just receive His love, I chose to love back, stay close to Him, and to obey even when it was difficult to do so.

Challenge: Deuteronomy 6:4-5 (NIV): . . . *Love the Lord your God with all your heart and with all your soul and with all your strength.*

Recite this scripture every morning and evening this week as a reminder of your desire to have a two-way love God through your praise, worship and obedience.

Notes & Reflections

In what ways can you worship God this week?

_____

_____

_____

_____

_____

Is there something you need to start or stop doing in order to be obedient to God?

_____

_____

_____

_____

_____

Love Changes Everything!

Week Four:
Love Yourself

Love Rejoices With the Truth

Love & Self Respect

We've looked at God's love for us and our love of God, but now we come to an aspect of love that's often more difficult—love of self.

What makes a high-powered executive woman succumb to an abusive relationship? Why does a woman return to her abuser or repeat abusive relationships? Why does a beautiful woman believe she's ugly? Why does any woman feel she doesn't deserve to be loved and cherished?

Because her confidence and self-image has been lost or damaged.

As we study the Bible this week, remember our past studies on how God views you: you are His beautiful child, deeply loved, and a person of purpose and possibility (just like your children are special and beautiful to you). If you don't love yourself, or even like yourself, I pray this week's study will help you understand why you feel that way, and how to restore a healthy self-image. This journey to healing begins by tackling three things that destroy our confidence: false perceptions, guilt, and shame. Believing *false perceptions* or *lies* strips you of confidence. *Guilt* is unproductive and often leads to depression. *Shame* leaves you stuck, blocking your road to restoration.

This is such an important lesson for most women, not just single moms. The more a woman has faced abuse, abandonment, rejection, ridicule, and verbal attacks, the easier her mind is trained to dislike—if not hate—herself.

Caroline came to me for counseling. After several weeks she said, "Every time my boyfriend and I get in a fight, I know just how it will end. He will pull out his gun and threaten to kill himself. That's our normal fight and how it will end. But that's not normal is it?"

She had lost all concept of normal, and she hadn't even considered he might turn the gun on her first, instead of himself. Believing his response was somehow her fault, the guilt that he might kill himself if she didn't give in and the shame of living like this had kept her stuck in a very dangerous situation. Sometimes we have to step away from the pattern of our life to see what's truth and what's become a destructive lie or lifestyle.

As we look at and apply scripture, your self-image can be transformed! This means your future behavior, goals, and life can look completely different than your past or present.

To love yourself in a healthy manner, you must discover the truth about who you are and then live out that truth with confidence. Let's being with the source of truth.

The Source of Truth

Love rejoices with the truth. This chapter on love involves finding truth, and to find truth we must rely on Scripture— the source of truth.

John 1:1 (NIV): In the beginning was the Word, the Word was with God, and the Word was God.

The Word is Jesus

John 1:14 (NIV): The Word became flesh and made His dwelling among us. We have seen His glory, the glory of the one and only Son, who came from the Father, full of grace and truth.

Jesus brought God's truth to us

John 17:17 (NIV): Sanctify them by the truth, your word is truth.

Sanctify means *to set apart, purify, entitled to respect.*

Jesus' words (Scripture) are truth

John 8:31-32 (NIV): . . . If you hold to my teaching, you are really my disciples. Then you will know the truth, and the truth will set you free.

When you study the Bible, you will find truth. This truth will set you free from the destructive and belittling lies that have controlled your past and present thoughts, choices, and self-image. God's truth will encourage, challenge and restore your confidence.

1.   *Where does real Truth come from?* [48]

_____

_____

2. *Where has your past "truth" come from?* [49]

_____

_____

3. *Which of these truths lead to hope?* [50]

_____

_____

FALSE PERCEPTIONS AND LIES

False perceptions keep us bound to sin, guilt, and unrealistic expectations. Their source wants to defeat, control, or manipulate. If it's coming from you, then it's become your defense mechanism against further hurts, or it's your excuse not to change.

> *John 10:10 (NIV): The thief comes to steal kill and destroy.*

Satan does this by making us believe we are worthless. Even the most beautiful woman cannot see her beauty when deceived by lies.

Truth is the opposite: we are free to expect, anticipate, and enjoy good things.

Check any of the behaviors or thoughts listed below that control your life, currently or in the past. These reactions to the emotional and physical pain we encounter in life are real, but believing you cannot change them is a lie.

- ☐ Having low self-expectations. You verbally speak negative words about yourself, don't believe you can succeed, etc.

- ☐ Feeling stupid: You don't think you can learn a skill or make wise choices.

- ☐ Feeling worthless. You feel empty of emotion or value.

- ☐ Self-pity. You are mired in your situation and repeatedly tell everybody your sad story without making any personal changes.

- ☐ Feeling guilt. You carry blame, whether something is your fault or not.

- ☐ Hating yourself. You hate who you are, or who you are unable to be.

- ☐ You compare yourself to others and always come up short.

- ☐ You see yourself as ugly or undesirable.

- ☐ Feeling stuck or powerless. You seem unable to change your family cycle, current circumstance, early home life, or lifestyle.

4. *Where did the thoughts that caused these behaviors originate?* [51]

_____

_____

Gloria put it this way: "I need God so that my life and the lies I have lived with since I was a little girl will no longer defeat me."

5. *Have you suffered from any of the things listed below because of these distorted beliefs?*

_____

_____

Body punishment: cutting, anorexia, bulimia, poor health choices

Addictions: alcohol, drugs, porn, sexual addictions, food

John 10:10 (NIV): . . . I have come that they may have life, and have it to the full.

6. *Who wants to give us life and joy?*

_____

_____

7. *What allows us to receive this hope?* [52]

_____

_____

John 10:11 (NIV): I am the good shepherd. The good shepherd lays down His life for the sheep.

8.   *Who loved us enough to die so that we can be loved and live in truth?* [53]

_____

_____

Let's begin our search for truth with this self-assessment and see how God can heal and restore a skewed or broken self-image.

Defeating Lies

Scriptures that will help you defeat destructive lies:

Lie: I'm ugly.

Truth: *I'm created in the image of God* (Genesis 1:27)

Lie: I'm stupid.

Truth: *We have the mind of Christ* (I Corinthians 2:16)

Lie: I'm worthless.

Truth: *While we were yet sinners, Christ died for us* (Romans 5:8)

Lie: I will never amount to anything.

Truth: *God has plans to prosper you and not to harm you, plans to give you hope and a future.* (Jeremiah 29:11)

Lie: I'm unlovable and nobody cares about me.

Truth: *Because of the Lord's great love we are not consumed, His compassions never fail, they are new every morning. Great is Your faithfulness.* (Lamentations 3:22-23)

God loves you!

Lie: Love means living in fear.

Truth: *Perfect love casts out fear* (1 John 4:18)

As we trust God, His love drives out our fears and He has shown us how to recognize a love that is not based in fear.

Lie: I'll always have a bad reputation.

Truth: *Salmon the father of Boaz, whose mother was Rahab...* (Matthew 1:5-6).

Rahab was a known prostitute (Joshua 2:1), yet in Matthew she's only known for being in the lineage of Christ. God restores our reputation when we live for Him.

Lie: I am defeated.

Truth: *The Lord is close to the brokenhearted and saves those who are crushed in spirit.* (Psalm 34:18)

You may feel defeated, but God wants to heal your brokenness.

When crushed, we lose self-respect and confidence, becoming hopeless and more vulnerable to abuse and manipulation. Believing we have value and are loved by God brings balance and health to our relationships, friendships, family, workplace, and home. God's love enables us to say "no" when necessary, without guilt or condemnation. It also establishes healthy boundaries, which help us (and our children) make better life choices.

> Grace had a tender heart, craved approval, and wanted to keep the peace at all costs. Over the years, her family used her sweet traits to enable their selfish and lazy lifestyles. She felt mean if she disciplined her children, unloving if she didn't cater to her husband, and was manipulated by both to get what they wanted.
>
> She felt loved when she served them, but was the brunt of anger or guilt when she did not. This was no longer a two-way love relationship but Grace couldn't see that. After her husband's sudden death, she began to discover God's truth. Her self-image was restored, and she then entered into a new, well-balanced relationship with boundaries and confidence. She is happily married today, no longer an enabler, dearly loved and respected by her husband.

In the following questions, don't confuse a bad behavior with a lie about who you are. For example: It may be true that you are, or have been, an addict, liar, alcoholic, angry, or bitter person. Those are behaviors God can help you overcome; they don't change who you are in His eyes! You are still a child of God, one He desires to bless and love, now and forever.

9. *What are the strongest negative thought(s) you've believed to be true about yourself?*

_____

_____

10. *How have they affected your life choices?*

_____

_____

11. *Can you now see how those names have dictated past behaviors?*

_____

_____

12. *Do you want to let these names or thoughts continue to control your life?*

_____

_____

If your answer is no, your journey to truth, self-respect and self-love has begun!

Guilt and Shame

Guilt is good when it convicts us of wrong behavior and motivates us to change. However, guilt is not a place to stay parked, nor is it appropriately applied after we have sought forgiveness. False guilt can also weigh you down when you take the blame for things that are not your fault.

Shame is dwelling on past mistakes. It doesn't allow you to forgive yourself, accept God's forgiveness, or begin a new life. It causes you to walk around with your head down, ashamed of who you are or where you've been. It can become an endless pity party, cause self-imposed isolation, or develop into a martyr attitude. Guilt and shame keep you stuck!

Some of our lives are messier than others. Some have made poor choices, while others have been victimized by the choices and behaviors of someone else. Regardless of how we got into our circumstance, God gives us a restart button, and a chance at a new beginning when we choose to follow Him.

> *2 Corinthians 5:17 (NIV): Therefore, if anyone is in Christ, he is a new creation, the old has gone, the new has come.*

13. *Is there a guilt or shame issue that has kept you away from God?*

   _____

   _____

14. *Has it kept you bound to destructive behaviors?*

   _____

   _____

15. *Do you believe guilt or shame has destroyed your self-image or limited your possibilities?*

_____

_____

16. *Why do you think a negative self-image hurts relationships?* [54]

_____

_____

Getting Rid of Guilt and Shame

Step 1: Ask for forgiveness. Accept God's forgiveness.

> *1 John 1:9 (NIV): If we confess our sins, He is faithful and just and will forgive us our sins and purify us from all unrighteousness.*

Repent means to turn away from our sins, not just say we are sorry for them. It means change. Seeking forgiveness purifies us by washing away our past.

> *Psalm 32:5 (NLT): Finally, I confessed all my sins to You and stopped trying to hide my guilt. I said to myself, "I will confess my rebellion to the Lord." And You forgave me! All my guilt is gone.*

King David confessed a huge sin, a life-changer for most of us. He had committed adultery with the wife of Uriah, a trusted friend and one of the "mighty men" who had pledged his loyalty to David. Then David had Uriah killed to try to cover up his sin. The baby of that sin died, however the son that David and Bathsheba later conceived was Solomon, David's successor to the throne.

God is about restoration, not condemnation.

> Psalm 103:12 (NLT): He has removed our sins as far from us as the east is from the west.

17. *How far away are our mistakes?* [55]

_____

_____

If you need to seek God's forgiveness, simply pray these words:

Father God, today I ask You to forgive me of my sins, all the things I've done wrong in life, for the people I've hurt, the way I've hated myself and others. Forgive me Father. I believe Jesus died on the cross to take away my sins, and I accept Your forgiveness. Fill me with Your love so I'm able to love myself, as well as others. Thank You Jesus for saving me, rescuing me from my past and setting me on a path towards the future You have planned out for me. In Jesus' name, amen.

Now, let it go!

> Proverbs 26:11 (NIV): As a dog returns to its vomit, so fools repeat their folly.

And don't return to it!

Step 2: Change your thought pattern.

Just embracing the fact that God loves you as His child will naturally begin the process of change.

Romans 12:2 (MSG): *Don't become so well-adjusted to your culture that you fit into it without even thinking. Instead, fix your attention on God. You'll be changed from the inside out. Readily recognize what He wants from you, and quickly respond to it. Unlike the culture around you, always dragging you down to its level of immaturity, God brings the best out of you, develops well-formed maturity in you.*

18.   *How do you renew your mind?* [56]

_____

_____

19.   *What badgering low self-esteem thought brings you down?*

_____

_____

20.   *Which scripture(s) will help you change your thinking?*

_____

_____

To find verses that will help you, learn how to use a Bible concordance. It's an alphabetical index of words, themes or people found in the back of most Bibles. It is a useful tool for finding verses on specific themes: loved, forgiven, thoughts, etc. You can also visit biblegateway.com or do an Internet search for "new creation scriptures" or another topic

> *Philippians 4:8-9 (NLT): And now, dear brothers and sisters, one final thing. Fix your thoughts on what is true, and honorable, and right, and pure, and lovely, and admirable. Think about things that are excellent and worthy of praise. Keep putting into practice all you learned and received from me— everything you heard from me and saw me doing. Then the God of peace will be with you.*

Focusing on positive attributes is the beginning of a changed thinking pattern.

> *Psalm 118:24 (NLT): This is the day the Lord has made, let us rejoice and be glad in it.*

List three positive things you can say about yourself now:

_____

_____

_____

I know changing your thought patterns is difficult, but it must take place to be rid of a dark or destructive self-image. A good self-image is key to self-love.

This week we've looked at how biblical truths can set you free from guilt, shame and destructive thoughts. Truth allows you to love yourself, regain self-respect, and walk in confidence. With respect comes a healthy expectation of how you deserve to be treated, so don't settle for anything less!

Can you now understand why "love rejoices with the truth"?

Challenge: This week say only positive words about yourself—all the time! Post "truth" scriptures around the house; keep them before you and say them out-loud to contradict the old destructive lies that enter your mind.

Notes & Reflections

What lie have you chosen to defeat this week?

_____

_____

_____

_____

What guilt or shame issue no longer controls you?

_____

_____

_____

_____

What scriptures have you chosen to memorize this week?

_____

_____

_____

_____

Love Changes Everything!

Week Five:
Love Your Enemies

Love Remembers No Wrongs

Love Those Who Hate You

Now that you have an understanding of God's great love for you, are expressing your love to Him, and learning to love yourself, it's time to love those who hate you and love those you hate!

I have purposely placed this week's teaching *after* establishing your love relationship with God and *before* establishing relationships with others. God's love empowers you to put your emotional baggage behind you so that hatred, bitterness and pain no longer impede your current or future relationships. I'll explain how through the scriptures we look at this week.

You are probably asking, "Why should I love *them*?" Let's look at scriptures to see what it means to love our enemies, and why loving *them* is important to *you*!

> *Luke 6:27 (NLT): But to you who are willing to listen, I say, love your enemies! Do good to those who hate you.*
>
> *Matthew 5:43-48 (NLT): You have heard the law that says, "Love your neighbor and hate your enemy." But I say, love your enemies! Pray for those who persecute you! In that way, you will be acting as true children of your Father in heaven. For He gives His sunlight to both the evil and the good, and He sends rain on the just and the unjust alike. If you love only those who love you, what reward is there for that? Even corrupt tax collectors do that much. If you are kind only to your friends, how are you different from anyone else? Even pagans do that. But*

you are to be perfect, even as your Father in heaven is perfect.

1. *Name one person you hate today. (If you're too nice to say you hate anyone, name the person who has hurt you the most with their words or actions.)*

    _____

    _____

2. *What one-word feelings or emotions did you have just thinking about them?* [57]

    _____

    _____

I haven't given you a lot of room to write, because I don't want you to dwell on them!

3. *Do you think your anger toward this person has affected other relationships in your life? If so, how? If not, why not?*

    _____

    _____

4. *How do you react or respond to this person when you must talk to them or be in their presence (words, temperament, behavior, body language)?*

    _____

    _____

5. *How do you react around others when this person's name or presence is involved (what are your words or emotions)?* [58]

_____

_____

Our reactions are often old learned behavior patterns. Your behavior is being dictated by a person you don't even like, which actually keeps you under their control! The person you "hate" may be out of your life, or even dead, but they still control your reactions to life.

> *Proverbs 25:21-22 (NLT): If your enemies are hungry, give them food to eat. If they are thirsty, give them water to drink. You will heap burning coals of shame on their heads, and the Lord will reward you.*

6. *How does being nice to your enemies benefit you?* [59]

_____

_____

Loving your enemy is about letting go of things from your past that still influence your current life. (If you are living with your "enemy," you must protect yourself and your family from destructive behaviors.) Being nice keeps you from becoming like *them,* but it does not mean you should allow (enable), or make excuses (give permission) for them to continue hurting you with their poor behaviors and choices.

If you do not want your life to be controlled by your enemy's words or actions, you must let go of the hurt, the past, and even their current intrusion into your life. This is not a feeling—it's a choice.

Make some new choices:

- Choose to change your attitude.
- Choose to forgive (we'll talk more about this later).
- Choose to protect yourself from further hurt.
- Choose to move forward with your life instead of looking back, wallowing, or feeding your anger.

Change Your Attitude

You cannot change someone else's attitude; so let that thought go too. You can only change *you*!

> *Romans 15:5 (NIV): May the God who gives endurance and encouragement give you the same attitude of mind toward each other that Christ Jesus had.*

With God's help we can change our attitude toward anyone. You "let go" when you give them to God. Let God deal with them, let God judge them, let God heal or condemn—It's His job, not yours!

> *Exodus 23:22 (NIV): If you listen carefully to what he says and do all that I say, I will be an enemy to your enemies and will oppose those who oppose you.*

Proverbs 16:7 (NLT): When a man's ways please the Lord, he makes even his enemies to be at peace with him.

Stay Positive

Ephesians 4:22 (NLT): Throw off your old sinful nature and your former way of life, which is corrupted by lust and deception.

7.   *What thoughts can you change toward the person you "hate"?* [60]

_____

_____

8.   *Consider at least one reaction you can change when confronted by this person in the future.* [61]

_____

_____

Choose to Forgive

To forgive means to "grant pardon," but it also means to "cease to feel resentment against."

Why should we do that?

The Bible tell us to forgive:

Matthew 6:12 (NIV): . . . forgive us our debts, as we forgive others.

Matthew 6:14 (NIV): For if you forgive other people when they sin against you, your heavenly Father will also forgive you.

Luke 6:37 (NIV): Do not judge, and you will not be judged. Do not condemn, and you will not be condemned. Forgive, and you will be forgiven.

Leave the judgment up to God!

Forgiveness releases you to live in peace:

Romans 12:17-20 (NLT): Never pay back evil with more evil. Do things in such a way that everyone can see you are honorable. Do all that you can to live in peace with everyone. Dear friends, never take revenge. Leave that to the righteous anger of God. For the Scirptures say, "I will take revenge; I will pay them back, says the Lord." Instead, if your enemies are hungry, feed them. If they are thirsty, give them something to drink. In doing this you will heap burning coals of shame on their heads. Do not let evil conquer you, but conquer evil by doing good.

Colossians 3:12-15 (NIV): Therefore, as God's chosen people, holy and dearly loved, clothe yourselves with compassion, kindness, humility, gentleness and patience. Bear with each other and forgive one another if any of you has a grievance against someone.

Forgive as the Lord forgave you. And over all these virtues put on love, which binds them all together in perfect unity. Let the peace of Christ rule in your hearts.

Forgiveness can improve *your* health! Even the Mayo Clinic has something to say about forgiveness and how letting go of grudges and bitterness can lead to a happier, healthier life: [62]

Letting go of grudges and bitterness can make way for happiness, health and peace. Forgiveness can lead to:

- *Healthier relationships*
- *Greater spiritual and psychological well-being*
- *Less anxiety, stress, and hostility*
- *Lower blood pressure*
- *Fewer symptoms of depression*
- *Stronger immune system*
- *Improved heart health*
- *Higher self-esteem*

Stephanie planned to drop her daughter off at a local church, go home to drink another beer, and then go and kill her sister. But God had a different plan for Stephanie that night. Instead, a determined woman from the church ran out to Stephanie's car when she arrived with her daughter, and invited her into church.

Stephanie wasn't dressed for church (PJ's), she wanted that beer, and she wanted revenge on her sister. Because one woman listened to the prompting of God, she rejected all of Stephanie's excuses. She coaxed her into the church and sat with her, and that night Stephanie gave her heart to the Lord. She has never been the same! She loves God, her little girl, her church, and is even best friends with her sister. God can soften and heal even hardened hearts and offer a new future when we give our anger and our enemies to Him.

We are no longer powerless or bitter women when we love our enemies. We make room for God to do His work when we get our anger out of the way.

Allison went to a single moms retreat filled with anger and bitterness toward her ex-husband and the woman he'd left her for. The day she arrived at the retreat, she received a call that her ex had died suddenly. Her emotions were very mixed since she still loved him, even though she hated how he'd hurt her. That evening Allison heard a message about forgiveness and the need to release past hurts for her own well-being. She chose to give her heart to the Lord and let go of her hatred.

The story doesn't end there. The next year she returned to the retreat with her ex-husbands widow. The woman who had been her enemy had now become her friend. The widow said, "I saw such a change in Allison after she attended this retreat. I told her I needed whatever it was she had found, and

I asked her to bring me with her this year". Both women were set free from bitterness and guilt and were able to pray together, let go of their past, and move forward with their lives in peace.

These women had good reasons to hate, but they chose to forgive. Because of that, they have new full lives, free from the control of their enemies, free to find joy, and free to have healthy new relationships.

Choose to Protect Yourself from Further Hurt

Matthew 10:16 (NLT): Look, I am sending you out as sheep among wolves. So be as shrewd as snakes and harmless as doves.

9.   *What does this mean for you?* [63]

_____

_____

Luke 9:5 (NIV): If people do not welcome you, shake the dust off of your feet as you leave the town, as a warning to them.

10.   *How does this apply to your enemies?* [64]

_____

_____

11. *Why is God sharing these verses with His disciples?* [65]

_____

_____

Choose to Move Forward

Philippians 3:13 (NIV): . . . But one thing I do: Forgetting what is behind and straining toward what is ahead.

Jeremiah 29:11 (NIV): For I know the plans I have for you," declares the Lord, "plans to prosper you and not to harm you, plans to give you hope and a future.

It's time to stop looking back and start looking ahead with a positive attitude.

12. *Have you given up on a dream or lost your way? Are searching for a new dream?*

_____

_____

Don't give up!

Matthew 19:26 (NIV): . . . with God all things are possible.

Psalm 147:3 (NIV): He heals the brokenhearted and binds up their wounds.

God does the impossible when He helps us forgive others and ourselves. He teaches us how to love our enemies so their behaviors no longer influence ours. He gives us new attitudes, better health, and positive thoughts as we choose to forgive. Seeking God's wisdom can protect us from further hurt in the future and enables us to let go of the past. "*Love remembers no wrongs*" —it's time to move on!

Are you now ready to remove hatred toward the enemy you listed in questions one from your life, and embrace a healthier future for yourself?

Challenge: Share with your group or write down one step you're choosing to take in order to love your enemies this week. Discuss how you want to react toward the person and report back next week.

Notes & Reflections

Memorize a verse that has helped you this week. Why did you choose this verse?

_____

_____

_____

_____

_____

Love Changes Everything!

Week Six:
Love Your Children

Love Always Protects

Love Is Patient. Love Is Kind. Love Always Protects.

NOTE: *This week is not about mistakes you've made or to enable guilt to overwhelm you. It's about growing in love, developing new parenting techniques, and breaking away from destructive generational patterns. If you've done things wrong, ask for forgiveness from both God and your child, and then move forward. God's forgiveness is immediate, but only He can soften your child's heart. Give them time. Also, keep in mind that you may do everything right, but a child still has the free will to make his or her own choices. We can teach and lead, but we cannot force good choices. If you have a rebellious child, fight the force that wants their soul, not your child. Pray, never give up, and stand firm.*

There are three specific aspects of "love always protects" that we will study this week: safety, discipline, and financial security. They are important in the healthy development of any child and will impact their future. If a child does not feel safe, has no boundaries, or lacks basic financial responsibility, he or she is unprotected against the world and will lack the skills required to succeed as an adult.

Even when we want to do the best for our children, it's sometimes hard to know where to begin. It's especially difficult if we were raised in an environment that didn't foster love, protection, or kind and patient discipline. We will once again look at scriptures to guide us towards a love that always protects.

PROTECTION in Your Home: Safety

Nehemiah 12:30 (NIV): When the priests and Levites had purified themselves ceremonially, they purified the people, the gates and the wall.

This story is about a man named Nehemiah and how he rebuilt the broken walls of Jerusalem. These walls were supposed to protect the people, the family of God. However, years of neglect, abandoning God, and disobedience had broken down the walls. Nehemiah had the vision to rebuild the walls so the Israelites would once again be protected. He faced fierce ridicule and opposition. The people worked with a shovel in one hand—repairing the walls, and a sword in the other—fighting the enemy. In the end, they sang songs of victory and celebration. They purified themselves and dedicated the gates and walls to the Lord. Many of us need to rebuild the broken walls of our homes today!

Sonja came up to me after a retreat and said, "I've been living with a man who sometimes is really nice, but other times he drinks and even does drugs. I love him, even though I'm afraid of him at times, but I don't know how we'd survive if I kicked him out. . . and it's so lonely to be alone."

Even the most loving mom can become vulnerable and unwittingly place her children in emotional or physical danger. Studies have shown fear, anxiety, and anger will affect a child's mental and physical development. When a child's safety is lost, frustration and anger build because they cannot protect themselves or the mother they love. I could list many statistics about children raised in fear-filled or abusive homes, but I'd rather focus on God's promises for those who turn their hearts to Him, repair their broken walls of protection, and live out their faith.

Leader Note [66]

1.   *Do you live in fear or on pins and needles?*

_____

_____

If yes, so do your children.

2.   *Do you deserve to be treated with care and respect, and do your children deserve a home without violence or fear?*

_____

_____

Remember Caroline from Week 4? She didn't even know when threats of suicide and violence had become her normal way of living. Caroline took action and made difficult decisions when she chose to rebuild her broken walls of protection.

Caroline's story may seem extreme, but I want you to see how cracked or broken walls of safety will only worsen if they are not recognized and repaired.

> Carrie's home consisted of a man she loved, alcohol, depression, and a gun. I received a call one night that Carrie had died. Was it suicide or was it murder? Though he was in the room with her, her boyfriend's story was suicide, but we'll never know. Either way, her walls had crumbled, she felt defeated, and she was left unprotected. Her children were away at the time, but still live with the after effects of an unprotected home and the loss of their mother.

Nehemiah recognized that the broken walls had left his people in a constant state of fear and defeat. He prayed for God's help and direction because he knew he couldn't rebuild the walls on his own. As you read Nehemiah 1:3-9, you'll see he prepared himself for the challenges he would face in rebuilding the walls. He prayed and fasted for God's direction. He sought forgiveness for his own sins and failures. He gained courage as he reminded himself of God's love and promises. His passion for a better future (rebuilding the walls) gave him the strength to face ridicule, temptations to quit, and attacks from his enemies.

Is it time to rebuild the broken walls of your home?

Nehemiah had a passion to restore hope and protection to his people. I love the book of Nehemiah because it takes an ordinary man on a journey that *changed the course of his people.* He overcame fear, resisted temptations, and did the impossible in record time because he knew God was with him.

3.   *Do you believe your home is always a safe place for your child?*

_____

_____

4.   *What would make your child feel unsafe?*

_____

_____

5.   *Do you allow potential danger into your home because of the friends you associate with? Examples: Drug users, those easily angered, or volatile, sexual predators (a man who expects, or demands sex from you).*

_____

_____

6.   *1 Corinthians 15:33 (NIV): Do not be misled: "Bad company corrupts good character."*

_____

_____

7. *Have your children ever expressed their fears either in words or actions?*

_____

_____

8. *How have you responded?*

_____

_____

9. *Do you still need to take action to make your home a safer place?*

_____

_____

10. *Do you need help to take this step?*

_____

_____

11. *Who is able to help you?* [67]

_____

_____

Loneliness is a real issue, but you must be choosy about your activities and friendships, especially those you bring into your home life. That is one purpose of a church family—to help build social and emotional bonds of friendship with one another in a safe and caring environment. Obviously, everyone who calls himself or herself a Christian does not live out that faith. We must learn to trust, but also be wise with our friendships. You learn a lot about a person from their friends, personal reputation, and history of integrity.

> *Hebrews 10:24-25 (NIV): And let us consider how we may spur one another on toward love and good deeds, not giving up meeting together, as some are in the habit of doing, but encouraging one another—and all the more as you see the Day approaching.*

I've emphasized unsafe relationships because that is a major factor for many single moms. However, an unprotected home can also include one that lacks proper meals, or educational supervision and allows unsupervised TV/Internet/phone usage or any other activity that leaves you or your children vulnerable to either abuse or failure.

Protection in your Home: Discipline

Remember boundaries *are* protection.

Harmful friends or relationships may not be an issue, but a lack of self-discipline or boundaries for your children can be just as destructive.

Not every single parent is from an abusive home. Many have come from great homes and wonderful families. Some have great parenting skills and support systems while others have no guidance or support—they may not even know where to begin. Some might say, "discipline is mean" because it was violently dispensed to you, while others know discipline is a display of love because it develops respect and responsible behavior when properly dispensed. The key to protecting our children is *how* we discipline and *what* boundaries we set.

Scripture is our best guide for self-discipline and for disciplining and preparing our children for adulthood.

Think about how each of these passages show love and how to protect your children?

> *Proverbs 22:6 (NIV): Train a child in the way he should go, and when he is old he will not turn from it.*

12.   *When is the best time to begin teaching our children godly principles?*

_____

_____

13.   *What promise and hope does God give us?*

_____

_____

> *Proverbs 13:24 (NLT): Those who spare the rod of discipline hate their children. Those who love their children care enough to discipline them.*

14.   *Discipline is an act of what?* [68]

_____

_____

A shepherd's rod or staff was not used to inflict injury on the sheep, but to guide them along their journey. It was used to direct the sheep, turn them away from dangerous paths, help them up when they were cast down, protect them from harmful predators, and lead them to peaceful pastures where they could grow in safety.

> *Proverbs 15:5 (NLT): Only a fool despises a parent's discipline; whoever learns from correction is wise.*

15. *What does discipline develop?* [69]

_____

_____

If you love your child, you must respond to inappropriate behavior; but a reaction is almost always harmful. A reaction is a spontaneous outburst usually filled with angry harsh words and excessive punishment. A response, on the other hand, means taking time to stop, think, and pray before responding.

> *2 Timothy 3:16-17 (NIV): All Scripture is God-breathed and is useful for teaching, rebuking, correcting and training in righteousness [healthy living], so that the servant of God may be thoroughly equipped for every good work.*

16. *What's our best parenting book?* [70] *Why?*

_____

_____

Hebrews 12:9 (NIV): Moreover, we have all had human fathers who disciplined us and we respected them for it.

17. What does discipline produce when it's properly dispensed? [71]

_____

_____

Ephesians 6:1-4 (NLT): Children, obey your parents because you belong to the Lord, for this is the right thing to do. "Honor your father and mother." This is the first commandment with a promise—so "things will go well for you, and you will have a long life on the earth." Fathers, do not provoke your children to anger by the way you treat them. Rather, bring them up with the discipline and instruction that comes from the Lord.

18. What helps a child honor their parent? [72]

_____

_____

19. Why is teaching respect of adults important for your child? [73]

_____

_____

Checklist: Your Discipline Methods Need Help If:

- ☐ You repeat threats of discipline but do not follow through.

- ☐ Your threats are unrealistic (you can't follow through with them).

- ☐ Your child gets their way because you tire of arguing.

- ☐ Your child feels entitled, pampered, or special to the point of expecting others to do things they should be doing themselves.

- ☐ Your child is ungrateful for gifts or kind gestures.

- ☐ You make excuses for your child's poor behavior, lack of responsibility, or selfish attitudes.

Checklist: Discipline Goals

20. *Give your child* **one** *warning, then follow through with a pre-arranged punishment such as time-out, loss of privilege, etc. Let there be no surprises or delays in punishment.* [74]

_____

_____

21. *Never threaten a punishment you cannot, or will not, follow through with.* [75]

_____

_____

22. *Follow through every time if you want to change behavior patterns.* [76] *This takes discipline on your part.*

_____

_____

23. *Keep their confidences and build trust, allowing for open communication especially when they truly need you.* [77]

_____

_____

24. *Be true to your word. This develops a sense of security.* [78]

_____

_____

25. *Teach responsibility and integrity.* [79]

_____

_____

26. *Circle one "help" and one "goal" from the lists above to work on this week.*

_____

_____

Lois' Journey: I remember when I began using these methods of discipline. After one short week, our chaotic home became calm. My kids knew what to expect, I had fewer outbursts of anger and frustration, and my children were learning that their choices garnered rewards or consequences. I was no longer the mean mom because they had to take responsibility for their own behavior. They are all hard-working adults today and have had favor in their jobs because they learned about choices and respect when they were young.

Protection in Your Home: Finances [80]

> *1 Timothy 5:8 (NIV): Anyone who does not provide for their relatives, and especially for their own household, has denied the faith and is worse than an unbeliever.*

The word "provide" in the Greek translation means to think beforehand, as well as to care and provide for.

Let's look at this verse in the financial sense of protection. This is about what you do with your money, not how much money you have.

Budget:

27. *Do you have a budget? If not, are you willing to have someone help you make one?* [81]

_____

_____

28. *Who can you ask to help you make a budget?*

_____

_____

29. *If you have a budget, do you live within it?*

_____

_____

Meals:

30. *Do you have a meal plan for the week that fits your budget?*

_____

_____

31. *Do you shop wisely to stay within your budget? (No impulse buying, junk food, pre-made meals that cost double and feed fewer people.)*

_____

_____

32. *Do you know how to cook meals form scratch, not just boxed/frozen meals?*

_____

_____

33. *Who could you ask to teach you better cooking skills?*

_____

_____

You can also Google "budget cooking" or "cheap healthy meals" to find many quick, easy, and budget friendly ideas.

Credit Cards:

34. *Do you carry a balance over each month on your credit card(s)?*

_____

_____

35. *Do you calculate how much interest you are paying each month on that unpaid balance?*

_____

_____

Usually 17% or more is added to the balance each month. Minimum payments will *never* payoff the debt.

Do you know someone who could advise you in paying off your credit cards?

If you can't think of anyone, ask those in your group, your pastor, or your local banker. Some banks have special programs to help single mothers.

Giving:

36. *Do you tithe to your church? (A tithe is 10% of your income.)*

_____

_____

Tithing is a principle that may not make sense, but amazingly God provides for those who tithe. (A tithe is 10% of your income.)

> *Malachi 3:8-10 (NIV): "Will a mere mortal rob God? Yet you rob Me But you ask, 'How are we robbing you?' In tithes and offerings. You are under a curse—your whole nation— because you are robbing Me. Bring the whole tithe into the storehouse, that there may be food in My house. Test Me in this," says the Lord Almighty, "and see if I will not throw open the floodgates of heaven and pour out so much blessing that there will not be room enough to store it."*

The New Testament also talks about tithing:

> *Matthew 23:23 (NIV): Woe to you, teachers of the law and Pharisees, you hypocrites! You give a tenth of your spices—mint, dill and cumin. But you have neglected the more important matters of the law—justice, mercy and faithfulness. You should have practiced the latter, without neglecting the former.*

Setting an Example

We set examples for our children with our own financial habits, work attitudes, and independence (or dependency):

- Speaking badly about an employer teaches disrespect.
- Try speaking words of gratitude for your job and see how your attitude changes.
- Seek more training or education to better your employment opportunities. Setting these examples will help your children to set goals, and seek unlimited possibilities for their future.

37. *Do you feel you are teaching your children to be successful in life?*

_____

_____

38. *How or how are you not?*

_____

_____

39. *Do you give your children the opportunity to think for themselves and make wise choices?* [82]

_____

_____

40. *Are you teaching them a good work ethic that will help them succeed in school and the workplace?* [83]

_____

_____

Lois' Journey: When I was young, I supervised two high school waitresses, Mary and Ginny. Mary made double or triple the tips that Ginny did. Ginny began to complain that Mary got the best shifts, or the best customers, and that's why she got such good tips.

I tried to explain to Ginny that they worked the same shifts and often had the same customers. The difference: Mary smiled, was friendly, and enjoyed serving her customers, while Ginny always looked stressed, or grumpy with her customer's requests.

Mary went on to become a nurse and had a great family; Ginny could never seem to succeed in her jobs or at life. Both girls came from difficult homes, but Mary's family taught her responsibility and respect and gave her hope for a better future, while Ginny's family stayed stuck in a generational pattern of self-pity. Ginny lacked a parental love that protected her from a life of failure.

List at least one step you can begin this week to improve your family's finances.

_____

_____

List the one help and one goal you set for better boundaries for your children.

_____

_____

List the one change you chose to make your home a safer place for your family.

_____

_____

You've written down goals this week to love your children in three specific ways: safety, discipline, and finances. Now it's time to pray and take action!

> Lois' Journey: I protected myself by isolating. Nobody, good or bad, could get into our life. But I couldn't rebuild my broken walls alone!
>
> It was a loving church family that replaced my walls of isolation and defeat with a wall of protection. I rebuilt the walls of broken discipline by setting new boundaries for our home. I got sound financial advice to help budget my meager funds. Our walls were rebuilt with a shovel—hard work and hard choices, and a sword—the Word of God that cut through my doubts, fears, and temptations to quit.

Challenge: Nehemiah didn't build the walls by himself either. Gather your team! You'll need people who pray, encourage, counsel, and work with you to rebuild your broken walls—*because love always protects.*

Notes & Reflections

What verse or thought do you most want to remember from this week's lesson?

_____

_____

_____

_____

_____

What impact did it make on you?

_____

_____

_____

_____

_____

Love Changes Everything!

Week Seven:
Love Your Friends

Love Does Not Envy

Jealousy and Dishonor Divide Friends

As single parents, we can sometimes drain our friends and family with our issues. Our problems blind us to the needs or feelings of those around us. If you are losing friends or having a hard time making new ones, it may be time to look at how you view and treat others.

Developing strong and lasting friendships takes work on our part. People tire of hearing our problems, listening to our excuses, watching us refuse advice, or being used in a one-sided friendship.

Answer the following questions honestly:

- Do I complain more than I converse with my friends?
- Do I listen to them and hear their heart, or just wait until I can talk again?
- Do I talk negatively about my friends to others?
- Do I talk to my friends negatively about others?
- Do I get angry when my friends do not respond to my need(s) quickly?
- Do I get angry when my friends give constructive (helpful) criticism about my behavior or choices?
- Do I honor my word (follow through with my commitments) to my friends?
- Do I honor my friend's schedules or find excuses for my tardiness?
- Do I recognize their pain or only see my own?

In other words, do you think about your friends' needs or only your own?

This week we are going to look at how to improve the way you love your friends. We need friends—different friends—because we have varied needs.

Do you have a friend who seems to bring joy to your life, even on a bad day or at the peak of your problems?

Do you have a friend who feels your pain but doesn't let you stay there? A real friend will listen and care but not feed your pain or anger with bitterness.

1. *Is there a friend in your life who keeps your confidences, prays for you, and prays with you?*

     _____

     _____

2. *Who's the dependable friend that you can call day or night in an emergency?*

     _____

     _____

Now let's reverse those questions and answer them *as the friend*:

3. *Am I a friend that brings joy into the life of my friends, even on a bad day or at the peak of my problems?*

     _____

     _____

4. *Am I a friend who feels their pain, but doesn't let them stay there? Do I feed their anger or*

bitterness, or do I try to help them overcome those feelings?

_____

_____

5. *Am I a friend who keeps confidences and prays for and with my friends?*

_____

_____

6. *Am I a dependable friend? Do I keep my word, follow through with my promises, and make myself available to help others?* [84]

_____

_____

Job 42:8-17 (NIV): My servant Job will pray for you, and I will accept his prayer and not deal with you [Job's friends and "comforters"] according to your folly. You have not spoken the truth about me, as my servant Job has." *... After Job had prayed for his friends, the Lord restored his fortunes and gave him twice as much as he had before . . . The Lord blessed the latter part of Job's life more than the former part.*

The book of Job is about a man who had one disaster after another strike him and his family. He suffered through the loss of his children, sickness, and finances. His friends began to speak badly about him and told him what a bad person he must be for God to let all these terrible things happen to him. His wife ultimately asks him, "Why don't you just curse God and die, Job?" These friends dishonored Job (and God) with their words, accusations, and assumptions. Today, friends who bring us down with their words of "comfort" are still called Job's Comforters—friends who actually do nothing to comfort us.

Even though Job did not understand why all these bad things kept happening, or why his friends turned on him, he would not turn on his friends or give up on his faith in God. In the end, God comes in and defends Job for his faithfulness, and Job prays for his friends, when he could have just been angry with them. God blesses Job because of his faithfulness.

Lois' Journey: I remember when my friends couldn't understand my situation, so they guessed and they gossiped, (haven't we all done that?), and almost all drifted away. Some stayed on the sidelines, but their attempted words of "comfort" unwittingly cut even deeper. They passed judgment without any knowledge.

My pain grew, my faith faltered, and my isolation deepened. Much like Job, I didn't have the energy to get angry with them and realized they couldn't possibly know what I was feeling. It took much longer than I liked, but eventually God restored my life and my friendships. He continues to bless me beyond my wildest dreams! I'm still meeting new people and making new friends all across the country.

Is it time to make amends with friends who just didn't know how to comfort you, were hurt themselves, or just made mistakes? As you forgive, God heals *you*.

Here are more examples of biblical friendships:

Confidant

> *John 13:21-25 (NIV): Truly, truly I tell you, one of you is going to betray me." His disciples stared at one another, at a loss to know which of them He meant. One of them, the disciple whom Jesus loved, was reclining next to Him. Simon Peter motioned to this disciple and said, "Ask Him which one He means." Leaning back against Jesus, he asked him, "Lord, who is it?*

John was close enough to lean in to hear the whisper of the Lord and receive information others did not.

Protector & Provider

> *John 19:26-27 (NIV): When Jesus saw His mother there, and the disciple whom He loved [John] standing nearby, He said to her, "Woman, here is your son," and to the disciple, "Here is your mother." From that time on, this disciple took her into his home.*

Jesus was on the cross when He transferred the care of His mother, Mary, into the hands of His closest friend, John. Because Jesus was the eldest son, He carried the responsibility to care for His widowed mother. Jesus made it clear to all that John was now "her son" and she "his mother" to meet the cultural requirements that would keep her protected and provided for.

Listener

> *John 21:4-7 (NIV): Early in the morning, Jesus stood on the shore, but the disciples did not realize that it was Jesus. He called out to them, "Friends, haven't you any fish?" "No," they answered. He said, "Throw your net on the right side of the boat." Then the disciple whom Jesus loved said to Peter, "It is the Lord!"*

Jesus appeared to many people after His resurrection, but they did not recognize Him. In this passage, Jesus spoke to the disciples from shore, telling them to cast their nets on the other side of the boat. It was only John who recognized the voice of the Lord.

Trust

> *Matthew 14:28-30 (NIV): "Lord, if it's you," Peter replied, "tell me to come to you on the water." "Come," He said. Then Peter got down out of the boat, walked on the water and came toward Jesus. But when he saw the wind, he was afraid and, beginning to sink, cried out, "Lord, save me!"*

Peter believed in Jesus enough to walk on the water with Him. He did well until he looked at the storm around him instead of Jesus.

Sharing and Without Envy

> *1 Samuel 18:4 (NIV): Jonathan took off the robe he was wearing and gave it to David, along with his tunic, and even his sword, his bow and his belt.*

David and Jonathan shared what made the other stronger. Jonathan gave David his military gear as a way of recognizing God's will for David to be King rather than himself. As the son of King Saul, Jonathan should have been the next king. Jonathan recognized God had chosen David over him and he showed no jealousy but rather support for his friend.

Ellen and Jane were two women following the voice of God. One was a single mom whose life had been a wreck, the other a loyal leader in several ministry roles. The leader befriended the single mom, becoming a mentor and encourager to her. In God's timing and plan, the single mom was given many ministry roles and opportunities the leader had hoped would be hers. Though it must have hurt, the leader never showed jealousy or spoke words of disdain. Though I'm sure she must have asked God, "Why 'her' and not me?," but she remained faithful where she served and never stopped praying for or encouraging her single mom friend.

7. *Do you give as much as you take in your friendships?*

_____

_____

Friendship over Evil

1 Samuel 19:1-3 (NIV): Saul told his son Jonathan and all the attendants to kill David. But Jonathan had taken a great liking to David and warned him, "My father Saul is looking for a chance to kill you. Be on your guard tomorrow morning; go into hiding and stay there."

Jonathan reminded his own father of David's faithfulness to him, but in the end protected David, his friend—the man God had anointed to become the next king.

Sacrifice

1 Samuel 20:4 (NIV): Jonathan said to David, "Whatever you want me to do, I'll do for you."

Philippians 2:3-5 (NLT): Don't be selfish; don't try to impress others. Be humble, thinking of others as better than yourselves. Don't look out only for your own interests, but take an interest in others, too.

Ruth 1:16 (NLT): But Ruth replied, "Don't ask me to leave you and turn back. Wherever you go, I will go; wherever you live, I will live. Your people will be my people, and your God will be my God.

Sacrifice is part of every true and meaningful friendship.

Lois' Journey: I was renting a home from my closest friends when my husband first left. They were charging me far below rental value so we could continue to stay there. Their personal finances suffered as they either broke even or lost money (in the winter months with heating costs) by renting to me, when they should have been making money on their rental property. This friend's sacrifice allowed my family to live in a safe home during a time of emotional and financial crisis. I'm grateful to this day for their friendship and amazing sacrifice.

Loyalty—Years after Jonathan's death. . .

2 Samuel 9:1, 6-7 (NIV): David asked, "Is there anyone still left of the house of Saul to whom I can show kindness for Jonathan's sake?" . . . When Mephibosheth son of Jonathan, the son of Saul, came to David, he bowed down to pay him honor. . . "Don't be afraid," David said to him, "for I will surely show you kindness for the sake of your father Jonathan. I will restore to you all the land that belonged to your grandfather Saul, and you will always eat at my table."

True friendship, according to the Bible, involves loyalty.

8. *Do you have loyal friends you can count on?*

_____

_____

When you have strong, healthy friendships, you've taken one more step toward a life of 1 Corinthians 13 love. You may need some personal counseling to help overcome some of the issues we've discussed. I encourage you to seek counsel from trusted leaders in your life, a pastor, or professional counselor. A word of caution regarding family: they are often not your best source of counsel because they do not easily forgive those who have hurt you. They may be too close to a situation to offer unbiased advice.

9. *If you believe you need personal counseling, how will you seek out help?*

_____

_____

10. *List three things you feel make you a good and loyal friend.*

_____

_____

_____

Bridgette was a struggling single mom trying to get her life together when she met Marilyn. There was over a 20-year age gap between these women, but somehow God brought them together. Bridgette had noticed Marilyn, now wheelchair bound due to Multiple Sclerosis, struggling to reach something on a shelf at their church. Bridgette simply asked if she could help and soon found herself taking Marilyn grocery shopping each week. Bridgette's help became invaluable; reaching products from top shelves, helping Marilyn checkout, loading and unloading her groceries, all the while listening to what Marilyn had to say about life. By taking a little time from her own crazy schedule to help someone else in need, Bridgette gained a new sense of life and hope. Marilyn and Bridgette both gained strength as they walked through their difficulties together instead of alone.

Challenge: Write at least one thing you've recognized this week that if changed, would improve your current or future friendships.

What first step will you take to bring about this change?

_____

_____

Notes & Reflections

I want to improve my friendship with:

_____

_____

By doing the following:

_____

_____

_____

_____

_____

Love Changes Everything!

Week Eight:
Love Relationships

Love Always Trusts

Trust Is Foundational

Our study today is about an intimate love relationship, which is something you may or may not even desire at this point in your life. However, this entire study is about a *life of love*, whether you marry or remain single.

Progression in love is the key. We all know you don't begin construction of a building with the penthouse. You begin at the foundation and build layer upon layer, strengthening each layer until you're ready to add the luxuries of the penthouse. However, in life we often want to start at the penthouse and then wonder why the foundation crumbles.

The foundation of love is God because *"God is love."* We build upon His love for us and on our love for Him, and then add layers of love to those we encounter in life. These loves prepare us for a healthy, loving relationship with a spouse.

This week is important because our human nature cries out to be loved!

> *Genesis 2:18 (NIV): Then the Lord God said,*
> *"It is not good for the man to be alone. I will*
> *make a helper who is just right for him.*

1.   *Do you desire to marry one day? Why or why not?*

_____

_____

You may have no desire to date or marry, and that's okay. The apostle Paul remained single because he chose to be fully devoted in his service to God. But he also realized everyone was not called to that same commitment.

1 Corinthians 7:7 (NLT): But I wish everyone were single, just as I am. Yet each person has a special gift from God, of one kind or another.

Lois' Journey: I've never remarried, yet I'm happy and content. I've certainly gone through times of loneliness (and still do), and I've longed to be loved by someone. But I also know my singleness has opened doors of opportunity and fulfillment that I could not have taken if I'd been married. I'm not certain that God always calls us to one or the other, but I believe He meets our needs in either place.

First Corinthians 13 comforts me as a single because I know this is how God loves and cherishes me. It has also taught me how to better love others and what a healthy loving relationship should look like. Should God have a different plan for me at some point, I feel He has prepared me—not for perfection but for love.

Whether you are seeking a spouse right now or not, this week is about being prepared for whatever relationships your future holds. It's about mending broken hearts, no longer living in the pain of your past, and living with healthy expectations for your future.

Trust in a Relationship

Trust doesn't come easily to single mothers. Once a person you fully trusted has betrayed you on an intimate level, walls go up. However, learning to trust is foundational for a healthy relationship. Once we begin to trust God, believing He truly loves us and wants the best for us, we can begin to gradually trust people again.

> *Psalm 13:5 (NIV): But I trust in Your unfailing love; my heart rejoices in Your salvation.*

> *Psalm 20:7 (NIV): Some trust in chariots and some in horses, but we trust in the name of the Lord our God.*

These are words of faith before facing a battle.

> *Psalm 28:7 (NIV): The Lord is my strength and my shield; my heart trusts in Him, and He helps me. My heart leaps for joy, and with my song I praise Him.*

These are words of faith in the midst of a battle.

> *Psalm 56:3 (NIV): When I am afraid, I put my trust in You.*

Even kings get scared.

> *Psalm 143:8 (NIV): Let the morning bring me word of Your unfailing love, for I have put my trust in You. Show me the way I should go, for to You I entrust my life.*

> *Proverbs 3:5 (NIV): Trust in the Lord with all your heart and lean not on your own understanding.*

Those words come from King Solomon, who is said to be the wisest man who ever lived.

2. *Can you fully love someone you don't trust?* [85] *Why?*

_____

_____

3. *Do you trust God?*

_____

_____

4. *How will a lack of trust in God affect your relationships?* [86]

_____

_____

Love is Not Self-Seeking

Love is not about having all of our needs met by a person, but it is about a mutual, two-way offer of love (God's example). There will be times when one side needs more than the other (illness, grief, etc.), but an unbalanced giving meter will eventually run dry. A 50/50 meter means you're only giving half of what you could be giving.

So how do we rid ourselves of selfishness in a relationship?

Take a look at almost any two-year-old. Their world is all about them. "Mine" is their favorite word, and possessive behavior toward toys, food, and mom are very common. It's the nature we are born with. A toddler needs to be constantly reminded by their parent to share, be kind, and think of others.

We can remain in a two-year-old mentality when over-indulged or constantly broken. Life becomes all about me: my needs, my wants, my way, or a "Help me, I can't help myself!" victim mentality.

We all need to be trained to be "good"—it rarely comes naturally. Even when present, goodness is attacked by the bullies and excluders of the world. We learn to fight and manipulate for acceptance because our human nature cries out to be loved. Or we give up and think we are unlovable, a lie that keeps us defeated and is a destructive burden on any relationship.

So how do we tame our human nature and take on the nature of God, with all of His characteristics and abilities to love selflessly, passionately, and with strength?

Fruit of the Spirit in Relationships

As Christ followers, we take on the nature of God through the Holy Spirit, and Scripture says we bear fruit from that nature.

Galatians 5:22-23 (NIV): But the fruit of the Spirit is love, joy, peace, patience, kindness, goodness, faithfulness, gentleness and self-control.

A fruit tree produces fruit from its own kind, and a healthy tree bears good fruit.

This fruit is something that should be seen in us as we follow Christ. But it's also something that should be seen in those we date or desire to be with. This fruit helps us judge the actions and intentions of others.

Matthew 7:20 (NLT): Yes, just as you can identify a tree by its fruit, so you can identify people by their actions.

5. *Which of the following characteristics have you used in the past to judge a person's character or intentions?*

   ☐ Emotional Connection

   ☐ Physical Attraction

   ☐ His Friends

   ☐ His Words

   ☐ How He Treats Others

   ☐ His Looks

   ☐ His Temperament

   ☐ Employment Record

- ☐ His Love of God (by his actions)

- ☐ How He Relates to Family Members

- ☐ Prayer and/or Advice from Your Friends

6. *How has using—or not using—these characteristics worked for you?*

_____

_____

7. *Have you included any of the following Fruit of the Spirit as a test of character?*

- ☐ Joy (Positive)

- ☐ Peace (Not argumentative)

- ☐ Patience (Not easily angered)

- ☐ Goodness (Honesty)

- ☐ Kindness (Sees the needs of others)

- ☐ Faithfulness (Trustworthy, follows through with promises)

- ☐ Gentleness (Understanding)

- ☐ Self-controlled (Eliminates destructive life-style behaviors)

8.   *Would using these qualifications have made a difference in your dating choices?*

_____

_____

You will see in the story below how a person exhibiting the Fruit of the Spirit in their daily life is better prepared for a relationship than one hanging on to a self-focused lifestyle.

> Melissa and Tom were in love. They had dated nearly two years, had a lot in common, and were on the brink of engagement. However, Melissa needed lots of attention, and wasn't happy if she didn't come first. She wanted Tom more and more to herself, isolating him from his family and friends. Tom finally realized how draining and one-sided their relationship had become and they broke up. Melissa dated several other young men over the years, but eventually the men broke it off. Melissa was beautiful, bubbly, and fun, but had not yet come to understand what selfless love was all about. Her human nature (selfishness) ruled above her Spirit nature.

When you are patient and prepared for a relationship, you allow God to bring you His best.

Several months after Tom's breakup with Melissa, Annie came into his life. Annie was a Christian, and had the same life goals as he did. Tom commented: "I didn't know relationships could be this easy or enjoyable. I now realize I was always on pins and needles with Melissa in an effort to make her happy."

Annie (and Tom) were motivated to find someone who complimented who they were, yet would challenge them to be better. They were not perfect people, but they were two people ready to give 100% to each other. The Fruit of the Spirit overruled their human nature of selfishness.

Motivation for Dating Relationships

Assess and check what drives your relationships:

- □ Sexual Desires

- □ Loneliness

- □ Financial Need

- □ Fear

- □ Desire to be "Rescued"

- □ Stress

- □ Companionship

- □ Social/Peer Pressure

These are realistic needs, but expecting any one individual to fully meet them is not.

God designed us to be loved and to love others. This is a natural human need, but it has been perverted by culture and society. Sex is mistakenly called love, and love is too often about self-gratification rather than mutual respect and sacrifice.

Compare the above list of "drivers" with the following names of God:

(Jehovah means the Lord—unchanging, eternal God.)

Financial Needs: Jehovah Jireh means "The Lord will provide"

Loneliness: Jehovah Rahfa means "The Lord who heals"

Sexual Desires: Jehovah-M'Kaddesh means" The Lord who sanctifies (makes us pure)"

Peer Pressure: El Shaddai means "God almighty –all powerful"

Fear/Stress: Jehova-Shalom means "The Lord our peace"

Companionship: Jehovah Rohi means "The Lord our shepherd"

These are just a few of the names of God listed in the Bible.

Once you trust God to be your provider, healer, strength, peace, and companion, you are ready for a relationship that will complement those traits. It will also bring you contentment as a single person, knowing God is forever at your side, able to meet your needs. Trusting in God gives you the self-confidence to use wisdom in your choices. A desperate, self-centered, or unhappy person will never be satisfied in any relationship.

Many women jump from one bad relationship into another out of fear, desire, or financial need. Notice the motivation behind Kim and Samantha's stories below.

Kim had been married twice. Her first husband went to jail and her second husband was an addict. She had three children, a lot of stress, and a great need to be loved. She fell for another man she wanted to marry. Her family and friends all told her to wait and get to know him better, but she refused to listen.

Against the advice of those who loved her, she married this man. He ended up being a manipulator, abuser, and thief. She was left broken and penniless, and her children became rebellious in their anger. Kim had been motivated by her emotional- and maybe sexual- needs, and she let them override her common sense and ability to listen to wise counsel.

Samantha was not happy with her home life. She desperately wanted someone to love her. She fell hard for the first young man who showed interest in her. She became pregnant at 17 by this young man, but then he left her.

Several years later, Samantha found herself with three children, three different dads, and still no husband. Her oldest child was a teen the last time I saw Samantha, and she was still unmarried.

Samantha had much love to give, but refused any boundaries. Her children lived in constant upheaval because of the men she brought into their lives, and they never found the love and security they all longed for. Samantha wanted God, but only when convenient and only on her terms. Her motivation in relationships remained selfish, and her nature remained rebellious.

9. *Can you see why the motivation for dating is important?* Why? [87]

_____

_____

10. *When you are properly motivated to date, will you now consider the background, history, and character of the men you choose to date?*

_____

_____

Wisdom in Dating Choices

> *Proverbs 18:15 (NIV): The heart of the discerning acquires knowledge, for the ears of the wise seek it out.*

The Spirit of God reveals the heart of a man, and good friends are wise advisers. Our hearts, when emotionally driven, can mislead us; however, God gives us discernment (the ability to see through deceit) when we seek Him.

11. *Have you asked God for wisdom regarding the people you date?*

    _____

    _____

> *James 1:5 (NIV): If any of you lacks wisdom, you should ask God, who gives generously to all without finding fault, and it will be given to you.*

> *Romans 12:2 (NIV): Do not conform to the pattern of this world, but be transformed by the renewing of your mind. Then you will be able to test and approve what God's will is— His good, pleasing and perfect will.*

12. *How can involving God in your choices protect you?* [88]

    _____

    _____

Hebrews 4:12—13 (NIV): For the Word of God is alive and active. Sharper than any double-edged sword, it penetrates even to dividing soul and spirit, joints and marrow; it judges the thoughts and attitudes of the heart. Nothing in all creation is hidden from God's sight. NIV

13. *Have you listened to the advice of your family or friends about the men you date?*

_____

_____

14. *Are they friends who care about your best interests and have made wise choices themselves?*

_____

_____

Psalm 1:1 (NLT): Oh, the joys of those who do not follow the advice of the wicked, or stand around with sinners, or join in with mockers.

15. *Have you argued with those who care about you, ignored your own common sense, or let your emotions take the lead?*

_____

_____

Proverbs 18:1 (NIV): An unfriendly person pursues selfish ends and against all sound judgment starts quarrels.

Are Your Children Ready for You to Date?

Just because you're ready to date does not mean your children are ready to accept a new man into your life or theirs. Choosing between your children and a new love will be a losing situation for everyone.

Are your children ready for you to date?

- What makes you think yes?
- What makes you think no?

Check the following characteristics that may describe your child:

- ☐ Feels the need to take care of you or protect you

- ☐ Wants to make you happy when you are sad

- ☐ Sleeps in your bed for comfort (either their comfort or yours)

- ☐ Takes on the stress of family decisions

- ☐ Expects, or is allowed, to be part of your conversations or activities with other adults

These are all signs that your child has become your emotional partner. Single mothers unintentionally give this "partner" role to their child when missing a spouse. This child is rarely ready to give up their position or their mother to a man. As you gain strength as a single parent, gradually reclaim your position of authority and caregiver to them. When you are secure and in control of your single parent home, you and your children will find contentment whether you date or remain single. [Note: Some children, even nonemotional partners, will never be ready for you to marry until they are grown—count the cost before you date.]

Is the Man You're Dating Father Material?

You must look beyond your personal, emotional, and physical needs to wisely judge the character of any man you bring into your life or home. It takes a special person to love another man's children. Check the list below:

- □ Can he deal with emotional or rebellious issues? (They may crop up later.)

- □ Will he be able to accept the role of co-father if the biological dad is in the picture?

- □ Is he a good example for your children? (This means he does not have abusive or addictive behaviors, is a responsible employee, and treats you with respect and care.)

- □ Is he patient or easily frustrated by their behaviors now? (Frustration only grows as normal family life and tensions crop up.)

- □ Are *you* ready to share the parenting role with him? Many single moms do not allow their new husband a voice, input, or the ability to correct the child's behavior. Are you both ready to share the parenting responsibilities? (If they remain "your children," they will not respect or accept him as a stepdad or husband to you. Children often pit their mother against their stepdad as a means of maintaining their position of power and control in the family.)

Does the Man You're Dating Have Children?

This is another issue that cannot be ignored. What's his role with his children? How will they interact with yours? Will they accept one another? Do not go blindly into a blended family. It can succeed, but it's an on-going effort that will require a lot of work, patience and probably some blended family counsel. (Resource [89])

Is your child comfortable around the man you are dating? Do not ignore the feelings of your children. If they do not feel comfortable around someone, listen—children have a sense that we don't. Children can't be forced to accept something or someone they are not ready for. It may take a year or two or ten. But again, if they are forcing you to choose between them and the man you are dating, it will be a loss for the entire family.

Purity in a Relationship

It's not easy to stay pure, and it's even harder to find a man that encourages you to do so. Once you've had a sexual relationship, it's hard not to desire it again, and the temptations are stronger.

16.   *Has sex kept you in a relationship that is harmful, dangerous, or just not right for your life goals?*

_____

_____

17. *Why do you think keeping a relationship pure makes a difference in its outcome?* [90]

_____

_____

18. *What are some ways to keep yourself and your relationship pure until marriage?*

_____

_____

Psalm 119:9-11 (NLT): How can a young person stay on the path of purity? By living according to Your word. I seek You with all my heart; do not let me stray from Your commands. I have hidden Your word in my heart that I might not sin against You.

19. *Have you noticed how any of the following influence the purity of your relationships?*

_____

_____

- The places and activities you choose
- Your mood (depressed, lonely, exhausted)
- The friends you choose
- Friends who help you to say 'no'
- Prayer

Sex is driven by emotions which often override wisdom, sound judgment, and common sense—leaving you in a dangerous or vulnerable position. Choosing to hold off on a sexual relationship allows time to accurately assess intentions, retain your self-esteem, and protect you and your children from further emotional or physical harm.

If a relationship is not kind, gentle or patient, if it envies or boasts, if it dishonors and is self-seeking, if it doesn't protect, honor or hope, and if it doesn't trust . . . then it is **not love** according to God's description in 1 Corinthians 13—and **it always fails**.

Fear in Dating

> *1 John 4:18 (NIV): There is no fear in love. But perfect love drives out fear, because fear has to do with punishment. The one who fears is not made perfect in love.*

Fear can keep us in a dating relationship that strips us of our personality and goals as easily as one that has destructive behaviors or abuse.

Have you feared being yourself in a past or current relationship?

> *Psalm 139:13 (NIV): For You created my inmost being; You knit me together in my mother's womb.*

God created you to be you, not who someone wants you to be.

Is there someone in your life right now who is making you stumble in your pursuit of God's character and "plans for good"?

> *Galatians 5:7-8 (NIV): You were running a good race. Who cut in on you to keep you from obeying the truth? That kind of persuasion does not come from the one who calls you.*

Fear of being alone forever is a real issue for most single moms.

20.   *Does your fear of being alone drive you to date — even the wrong person?*

_____

_____

> *Isaiah 54:5 (NIV): For your Maker is your husband, the Lord Almighty is His name— the Holy One of Israel is your Redeemer; He is called the God of all the earth.*

> *Hebrews 13:5-6 (NIV): Keep your lives free from the love of money and be content with what you have, because God has said, "Never will I leave you; never will I forsake you." So we say with confidence, "The Lord is my helper; I will not be afraid . . ."*

It's not easy to be alone, but dating out of fear of being alone is not the right motivation. A relationship should enhance your life, not be the substance of it. Don't be afraid to be choosy!

Angela found herself divorced and a single mother, something she never thought would happen. Although she wanted to be married again, she didn't rush at the first man that came her way. She went through the healing process needed to stand strong as an individual woman and mother. Then she began to pray that God would send her a new husband.

Several men wanted to date Angela, and although they were good men, she knew they weren't right for her. After a while, her job forced a cross-country move, away from her potential suitors. But God had her man 1,000 miles away.

When she met Clint, Angela knew he was the one God intended for her, and they've been happily married for several years. Angela was patient. She didn't fear being alone, but trusted God for her future. Fear didn't cut short her career or her chance at a new life—and the right husband.

21. *Are you currently in a relationship that is based on some type of fear?*

_____

_____

22. *What is the fear driving it, (loneliness, abuse, finances, etc.?)*

_____

_____

23. *Do you need to consider breaking off a relationship, even for a time, until you can enter it without fear as the foundation?*

_____

_____

Ask your friends—or those in this group—to pray with you for wisdom, timing, and dating choices.

Fear can also isolate you from any meaningful relationships, which can be just as destructive as entering into bad relationships. It deepens sorrow, prolongs grieving, takes away joy (because we live in fear), and can harden our hearts.

> Shawna's husband had divorced her. She had done everything she knew to please her husband, but it just wasn't enough. In the process of trying to always make her husband happy, she lost herself. When left alone, she shriveled up. She didn't know what made her happy anymore. Activities, goals, cooking—everything she'd done in the past had been things that pleased her husband.
>
> It took Shawna a couple of years to finally rediscover things she loved to do again, but

she refused to date anyone. Shawna feared a repeat of her first relationship, the pain of losing someone she loved again, the inability to make anyone happy, and the loss of herself in the process. Fear caused her to avoid all relationships. It took Shawna a long time to realize her fears had stolen her joy, ability to love, desire to set new goals, and a future filled with possibilities.

Your Readiness to Date

We've looked at the characteristics of those you might date. Now let's see where you rank on the dating scale.

- ☐ Are you trustworthy?

- ☐ Are you honest or do your fears cause you to lie?

- ☐ Are you patient?

- ☐ Are you easily angered?

- ☐ Are you emotionally needy – are you looking for someone to "rescue" you?

- ☐ Are you disciplined in your sexual life or swayed by a touch or desire?

- ☐ Are you unforgiving, still holding grudges?

- ☐ Are you kind, patient, and gentle?

- ☐ Are you dependable and faithful to your word?

☐ Do you have joy?

☐ Are you at peace with yourself and others?

Nobody will check off everything on this list because we all struggle with personal issues throughout our lives. However, if you are struggling with several, a few, or only one of these issues, ask God to begin your healing, strengthening, and renewal.

God knows our hearts can be broken and our spirits (the will to live) crushed, but He doesn't want us to remain there. He has answers and hope for the days ahead.

> *Psalm 147:3 (NIV): He heals the brokenhearted and binds up their wounds.*

> *Psalm 34:18 (NIV): The Lord is close to the brokenhearted and saves those who are crushed in spirit.*

You may need to seek out counseling for some issues you circled above. Just begin to conquer the things that have hurt your past relationships so they won't affect your future ones.

24.   *Why is healing from our past important in living a life of love?* [91]

_____

_____

25. *Now that you've done this study, what old attitudes or behaviors would you eliminate in a new relationship?*

_____

_____

26. *What new healthy attitudes, behaviors, or boundaries would you bring to a future relationship?*

_____

_____

27. *Do you trust God and believe He has your best interest at heart?*

_____

_____

28. *Do you trust yourself to make good choices?*

_____

_____

29. *Are you in a place to give—not just receive—in a relationship without sacrificing your personality or the current and future needs of your children?*

_____

_____

30. *Which rules more of your life today—your human nature and emotions. or the Spirit of God with the Fruit of the Spirit being evident?*

_____

_____

31. *Has anything changed in your motivation to date since you began this week's study?*

_____

_____

32. *If yes, what has changed?*

_____

_____

33. *Do you believe you can use wisdom and listen to wise counsel regarding your dating choices at this time?*

_____

_____

34. *Is fear a current factor in your relationships?*

_____

_____

35. *Do you feel you're able to stand up for yourself and be choosy about the men you date?*

_____

_____

This week, if you've been honest with your answers, you should have a better idea if you're ready to date, be content in singleness (even for a time), or dissolve a relationship that is either not healthy or just not God's best for you.

36. *Do you believe you are ready to begin a serious relationship at this point of your life? Why or why not?*

_____

_____

37. *If not, are you now better prepared to wait?*

_____

_____

No relationship is perfect, as no person is perfect. However, I hope this week you've seen that God gives us boundaries and equips us to work together in our relationships as we *trust in Him.*

Challenge: If you're in a group study, pray together for strength to wait, to stay pure, and listen for the voice of God. If someone needs to break off a relationship, stand together in prayer and get outside direction if it's a dangerous situation.

Notes & Reflections

What was the most important thing you learned this week about relationships?

_____

_____

_____

_____

_____

Love Changes Everything!

Conclusion

You've just spent eight weeks learning about love from God's perspective and how to live out that love in all of your relationships. I hope you have come to believe God deeply loves you, desires a relationship with you, and has the power to generate His love through you to others. His love sets you free from your past and gives you the opportunity to live a new and better life of love.

This journey of love and its challenges will never end because people will try your patience, make you angry, remind you of your mistakes, and let you down. *But God will not.*

A few closing thoughts and challenges to keep you on track...

Reminder:

> *1 John 4:17 (NIV): And as we live in God, our love grows more perfect.*
>
> *James 4:8 (NIV): Draw near to God and He will draw near to you.*

Daily Prayer: God, I thank You that You love me on both my good and bad days. I ask You to fill me with Your love today so that I'm able to love myself and others with Your love—even when I'm tired, angry, frustrated, or just don't feel like it.

Challenge: Review the weeks you need the most, pray for God's guidance, be encouraged by the scriptures, trust Him more each day, and allow the fruit of the Spirit to flourish in your life.

Goals: Receive God's love, love God, love yourself, love your enemies, love your children, love your friends, and live a life of love—whether in a relationship or as a single adult.

Notes & Reflections

_____

_____

_____

_____

_____

_____

_____

_____

_____

_____

_____

_____

_____

_____

_____

_____

_____

_____

Because Love Changes Everything!

About the Author

Lois has over 20 years of experience as an ordained minister, pastor, church planter and missionary. She speaks nationally at single mom gatherings, women's events, leadership seminars, and church services. Having raised 5 children as a single mother herself, she knows what it's like to feel afraid, overwhelmed and hopeless. Her books and articles are written to encourage single mothers and train leadership.

You can follow her ministry at www.loisbreit.com.

Other works by Lois:

30 Days of Choices

Single Mom Ministry:
Church Leadership Guidebook

Answers and Leader Notes

(Endnotes)

Week One:
Love Revealed

1—Some single moms are very confident in their ability to be loved and to love others. However, for those who have been abused or rejected, it's easy to lose self-worth. Some even accept abusive behavior as acts of love. Others think kindness and/or sex means love.

2—There are no right or wrong answers. This is a personal feeling, though as we continue our study, you will discover those feelings may not be truth. Just answer truthfully as we set the stage for learning about love.

3—God created you, gave you your personality, strengths, form —nothing about you is hidden from or a surprise to Him. He loves you because He chose to create you! His love is not based on how someone has treated you or what they've said to you, but on the fact that you are His child, created by Him out of love, and therefore you are special to Him!

4—We are His children, lavished (spoiled) by His perfect love, if we accept it.

5—The son made the choice to return to the father and sought forgiveness, expecting nothing, but receiving his father's love and acceptance.

6—Another reminder that nothing we have done can separate us from God's love. Its always there waiting for us to grab on to, respond to, and act upon.

7—Have faith/believe and repent. God loves all of us, whether or not we choose to love Him. However, we miss out on the many blessings He has for us when we reject His love.

8—God does not have a human nature (selfishness, frailties, or ability to make mistakes). We can make mistakes as a parent, but God cannot.

Week Two:
Your Love for God, Part I

9—David is ridiculed for praising God after a great victory. Michal, his wife, is embarrassed by David's unashamed singing and dancing as he praised God—maybe even jealous of his love for God.

10—God and David's relationship continues to be joyous and close, while Michal is left barren.

11—We too are 'barren' (empty) when we are unable to praise or love God.

12—David is under personal attack—in need of help.

13—God rescued him and brought victory against his enemies.

14—God is in control and rescues us in times of trouble.

15—The promised temple is completed.

16—A sanctuary where all the people could praise and worship God is established.

17—We remember God's promises and that He is faithful to fulfill them!

18—They are facing an overwhelming army/battle.

19—Songs of praise (confidence) went before them, reducing fear.

20—Peace was attained when praise came first.

21—David needed guidance from God.

22—God will reveal His will and instructions to us as we seek and praise Him.

23—God answers our questions and solves our problems, even in our sleep, when we have been praising Him.

24—When sinful and afraid . . .

25—Strength and joy replace fear and condemnation.

26—God is merciful; with repentance and praise comes joy.

27—David is depressed.

28—Hope was restored through his praise.

29—God is with us even in the dark times. Praise restores hope.

30—David is being pursued by King Saul who has sent men to David's house to kill him.

31—David is once again spared and protected by God. (David never stops praising Him.)

32—Powerful or deceitful men (lawyers and liars) are not mightier than God.

33—The trouble continues—David went through a long period of harassment and hateful attacks.

34—Praise is a reminder of God's past and present acts of loving faithfulness to protect and bring victory.

35—Keep praying— victory will come!

36—Your answer should include some of the following: focusing on the good in others; not focusing on blame, but on God's ability to bring you through; praising God keeps hate from taking over; David didn't hate Saul though Saul was trying to kill him; David praised God for His ability to deliver him; praise brings victory!

Week Three:
Your Love for God, Part II

37—The answer should include: being in God's presence restores a peaceful attitude; He will deliver you from problems; realize God is in control, not you; blessings follow, as we worship God; be humble, not arrogant; it makes me a better friend, parent, and mate because it makes me easier to get along with and more aware of others needs.

38—Obedience brings blessing.

39—Life.

40—Provision

41—Truth gives us power to change our lives.

42—Wisdom, and it protects our heart from evil.

43—Love and obedience are partners

44—Answers could include some of the following: blessings, life, wisdom, trust, protection, power of truth, love.

45—Sorcery, witchcraft, opposition to God.

46—Without obedience there is no respect; blessings are withheld, trust is impossible.

47—It shows respect, which develops trust, insures the flow of blessing, and solidifies a two-way relationship.

Week Four:
Love Yourself

48—The Word of God/Scriptures

49—Your family, friends, enemies, and culture (TV, books, ads).

50—The Bible because it never changes, it's constant and timeless. The Bible's Truth is God's description of His love and it reveals His promises for you. It encourages, gives hope, challenges, and betters us.

51—Distorted, cruel words spoken by friends, family, or enemies can take over our thought life. Their words become our truth, even when they are lies about who we are (children of God). Remember truths about our past behavior are not true for our future.

52—Biblical Truth, choosing to accept God and His love

53—Jesus is the Good Shepherd

54—We don't feel we deserve to be treated well, loved or cherished when we feel guilty about our past. We are unable to love others in a healthy way because we are trying to compensate for all our negative self-perceptions. Guilt destroys our self-image. It limits our possibilities and how we relate to others in relationships.

55—They are out of sight, they are gone forever.

56—By reading and trusting God's Word about who you are and setting new goals instead listening to your unhappy friends, unhealthy magazines, or unrealistic TV shows.

Week Five:
Love Your Enemies

57—Anger, resentment, hurt, avoidance, ambivalence

58—Angry or bitter words, re-tell your story, withdrawal, etc

59—When you show kindness, it stops you from becoming like them—their behavior looks foolish, not yours.

60—For example: when you think of them, give them to God and let it go; don't dwell on them; if you're confronted by them, pray to stay calm and remain silent until you are ready to respond; try not to be reactionary.

61—Examples: stay calm; smile, don't sneer; refuse to be sarcastic or caustic.

62—"Forgiveness: Letting go of Grudges and Bitterness" *Mayo Clinic.* Mayo Clinic, 11 Nov. 2014. Web http://www.mayoclinic.org/healthy-living/adult-health/in-depth/forgiveness/art-20047692

63—We have to go out and live in the world, but God gives us wisdom to recognize harmful situations (and people). A serpent is wise, has keen eyesight, and is quick to learn. A dove is harmless and gentle. So remain gentle, but learn from past experiences.

64—Not everyone will be your friend; don't try to change others; don't hang around them; move on to better people, places, and activities. Get out of harm's way.

65—Because he wants them to be pure in heart but prepared and strong; not easily hurt or offended or turning to anger, revenge or poor reactions. He wants to protect them from falling into traps and to stay away from those who desire to harm them. He advises them to shake off rejection, stop fretting, and move on to the next thing (or people) God has for them.

Week Six:
Love Your Children

66—These are resources for statistics on children in unsafe homes: Kidsdata.org, americanspcc.org

67—If you don't know anyone who can help you, ask your pastor or social services worker for guidance in making your home a safer place. They may refer you to someone who can help, or the church may be able to help you. Either way, take that first step toward "love always protects".

68—Discipline is an act of love. We must let our children know there are consequences to inappropriate behavior, but our response must be appropriate. A discussion with a two-year-old is futile, but a time-out or lost privilege teaches them boundaries in behavior. Lost privileges speak loudly to teens.

69—Wisdom

70—The Bible - Because it teaches us godly responses to difficult situations and equips our children for life.

71—Respect

72—Teach them the love of God in all that you do and say. Don't put unrealistic expectations on your child, or use extreme punishments.

73—Respectful children succeed in school, with friends, and in their jobs. Disrespectful behavior develops selfish or entitlement attitudes, rebellious behavior, and condescending relationships.

74—Give them one warning with a choice to obey, or receive their pre-arranged punishment (time-out, loss of privilege, etc.). If you give two or more warnings, you've lost control of the situation. When you follow-through every time, they learn quickly you mean what you say.

75—Don't let your anger or frustration take charge. Consider the cost of your threat (to you, as well as your child), and if you can or will be able to follow-through. Can you leave the store, restaurant; will you keep them from a party or event; think before you speak so your words are valid.

76—Follow Through: This takes discipline on your part. You will have to get off the sofa, off your phone, stop your car (don't try to punish while driving), leave a store . . . Without follow-through they will continue to push your buttons, get their way, and lose respect for you and your authority as a parent.

77—Refrain from talking about your child's bad habits or behavior with others. Your child will know if you are doing this and will lose trust in you. Trust is crucial as they enter the teen years. Find a prayer partner who keeps confidences to pray with you for specific needs.

78—This also means self-discipline on your part. I often see parents committing to an activity and then changing their mind at the last minute. To build trust, respect and security, follow-through with planned events, even if you're not in the mood or have poorly planned your day. Singles are notorious for last-minute commitments, but you are no longer just single, you are a parent with a little life depending on you to fulfill your word to them. Security and trust are built when you are true to your word.

79—Do you feel you're teaching your child to become a mature adult who will take responsibility for their personal actions, instead of making excuses for them or blaming others?

80—Because I cannot cover all the financial information in this space, I'm listing some resources: Larry Burkett (money management books for young couples, adults, teens); Dave Ramsey (Financial Peace University, books on financial planning).

81—It's pretty easy. Your expenses cannot exceed your income. If they do you need help to adjust your living and spending habits to do so.

82—If not, you can begin by giving them two or three options when they have choices to make, and also by not making every decision for them. Let them fail in the little things so they learn how to make wise decisions when the important things come along.

83—Are you on time for your job? Are you a dependable employee, trusted, taking steps to improve educationally, or by on-the-job training? Children watch and copy our behavior more than they listen to our many words.

Week Seven:
Love Your Friends

84—If you are not a good and dependable friend, it will be very difficult to make good friends. Friendships, like all other relationships, must be two-way in order to succeed.

Week Eight:
Love Relationships

85—No, because you will always be waiting for the betrayal, the lie, the insincerity. You may love them, but not fully because your guard is up and your expectations are low.

86—If you do not trust God first in your life, you will not have His joy, expect His blessings, or experience His peace. You will put all these expectations on a boyfriend or spouse who will constantly disappoint you. Nobody is able to meet all our emotional needs, except God.

87—If your motivation is to be rescued, you'll take the first person showing an interest in you. If it's rebellion, you'll continue to want your way and find yourself alone. If it's fear, you'll continue to find domineering or controlling partners.

88—No man will be able to meet all of your needs. You need to have God as your foundation, being dependent upon Him. Then a man can add to your life not be the sum of it.

89—www.familylifeblended.com

90—If not pure, but sexually driven: The relationship is based on a physical attraction, which eventually fades. The desire for sex is stronger than the desire for what's best for you and your children. It destroys your ability to see long term. Sex is designed to come after the commitment of marriage because it's designed to seal a commitment, not form one. When the order is reversed, self-gratification is the foundation, not commitment to the person. God gave boundaries to our sexual lives for our emotional and physical protection, not to deny us its pleasure.

91—You don't want to repeat past mistakes or destructive behaviors, or bring unrealistic expectations into your future.

CPSIA information can be obtained
at www.ICGtesting.com
Printed in the USA
LVHW041800160420
653682LV00012B/1879